CATFISH

Kevin Maddocks

Beekay Publishers

Other angling titles by Beekay Publishers:

Coarse

Carp Fever by Kevin Maddocks
The Art of Pole Fishing by Dickie Carr
Pike Fishing in the 80's by Neville Fickling
Basic Carp Fishing by Peter Mohan
Modern Specimen Hunting by Jim Gibbinson
Top Ten – tactics for the major species from ten leading anglers
Edited by Bruce Vaughan
Redmire Pool by Kevin Clifford & Len Arbery
Tactics for Big Pike by Bill Chillingworth
In Pursuit of Carp & Catfish by Kevin Maddocks
Cypry The Carp by Peter Mohan
The Beekay Guide to 450 Carp Waters
Jim Davidson Gets Hooked by Jim Davidson
In Pursuit of Predatory Fish by Neville Fickling
Tiger Bay by Rob Maylin
Understanding Barbel by Fred Crouch
Big-Water Carp by Jim Gibbinson
Mega-Pike by Eddie Turner

Sea

Boat Fishing at Sea by Phill Williams & Brian Douglas
Long Range Casting & Fishing Techniques by Paul Kerry
Cod Fishing by John Rawle
Uptide & Boatcasting by Bob Cox

Game

The Colour Guide to Fly Tying by Kevin Hyatt
Robson's Guide to Stillwater Trout Flies by Kenneth Robson
Dressed to Kill by Bob Carnill & Kenneth Robson

First published in 1990 by
BEEKAY PUBLISHERS
WITHY POOL, BEDFORD ROAD,
HENLOW CAMP, BEDS. SG16 6EA

© Beekay Publishers 1990

Typeset by BP Integraphics Ltd., Bath, Avon
Printed in Great Britain at The Bath Press, Avon

ISBN 0 947674 33 0

Contents

Photographs by the author and friends.
Drawings by Len Gurd.

when on the bank.

The wels is not indigenous to this country—nor is the carp, for that matter: and the first successful stocking took place on 27th October 1880 when about 70 'cats' were put in the Shoulder of Mutton Lake, at Woburn Abbey, in Bedfordshire.

Other unsuccessful stockings took place before this. In 1864 Sir Stephen Lakeman imported 36 Danubian wels from Bucharest, Romania but there was no signs of the 14 survivors that he released at Aldermaston Park, Reading when the lake was drained three years later. One can imagine Sir Stephen's disappointment especially as he'd accompanied the catfish throughout their 1800 mile journey!

Sir Joshua Rowley was next to try in 1865 by stocking wels into a lake connected to the River Stour near Flatford Mill. Surprisingly, in 1894, some 29 years later, a catfish of around 30 lbs was caught from the river at Flatford. Unfortunately, nothing more has been heard or seen of the Stour catfish and one can only assume that they never bred.

The Marquess of Bath stocked a few small wels into his lake near Frome in 1872 but three years later the lake was drained to find only three remaining fish. The two biggest were sent to London Zoo and weighed 28 and 18 lbs, the third one suffered gas mark 4!

After the 1880 stocking, little was heard of the Woburn cats until around 1950, as the Duke of Bedford's Estate was very private in those days, and little fishing was allowed. By 1951 it was felt that some of the Woburn Lakes had become overcrowded, and many fish were removed. It is a recorded fact that some very large catfish were killed because it was feared that they were eating some of the water birds. Unfortunately, most were not weighed accurately, but from the descriptions it seems possible that some of the catfish killed were probably over 60 lbs in weight (it is rumoured that one was 78 lbs and measured 6 feet in length)—remember they are a long-lived species that had lived undisturbed in the lakes for many years.

Leighton Buzzard Angling Club and Dawley Angling Association, which helped to net the fish, were given some of the smaller 'cats' and these went into Claydon Lake, in Buckinghamshire, and into Withy Pool at Dawley in Shropshire. In the fifties catfish to 20 lbs. were reported from the Dawley water topped by a 29 pounder in the 60's. By 1961 the catfish record stood at 33 lbs 12 ozs and had been taken from the middle lake at Claydon, by Reg Hutt. Catfish soon started to turn up in other waters in the area, to which they had been introduced by anglers taking them from Claydon where at one time they were not wanted by the club. Woburn Sands, Ledburn Pit, Snowberry Lake, Jones Pit and Tiddenfoot Pit all received stockings in the 60's. Tring Reservoirs, not so far from Woburn, were the first to produce a really big catfish following a small stocking of large wels into Marsworth Reservoir in 1907 by the

This Marsworth catfish, estimated to weigh about 40 pounds was found dead in 1934. Holding the fish are C. E. Double, grandfather of the present Tring bailiff, and T. Plumridge. The catfish, plus another found dead in 1943 and estimated to weigh 50 pounds was almost certainly one of the originals stocked in 1907.

Rothschild family. The British Record was eventually beaten in 1970 by a fish of 43½ lbs taken accidentally by Richard Bray whilst pike fishing at Wilstone Reservoir, part of the Tring complex. It is interesting that this big fish came from Wilstone and not Marsworth. In 1928 a four pound catfish was caught from Marsworth proving that a breeding population had been established and it is probable that some small ones found their way through the pipe which connected the two reservoirs. If this was not the case then anglers were responsible and several have admitted to stocking Startops Reservoir, the other main water in the group, some years ago. One thing that's not in doubt is that more than one catfish found its way into Wilstone; the 43½ pounder unnecessarily perished when someone had a 'brain wave' to deliver it to London Zoo, yet in 1990, CCG member, Kevin Hampton made angling history by landing another Wilstone cat of 39.6 which this time was returned safely to the water. It is interesting to note that a 5 foot catfish, estimated about 40 lbs, was found dead in Marsworth in 1934 and a second fish weighing about 50 lbs was also found dead in 1943; both of these were probably original fish from the 1906 stocking. Since then, no large fish

One of Kevin's greatest angling achievements – the first ever catfish caught intentionally from the Tring reservoirs in 1984.

had shown in Marsworth and it wasn't until 1984 that the first intentionally-caught catfish were produced by Bob Baldock and myself—we caught five cats in the 21½ to 4lb range. In 1989 a double was caught in Marsworth and in 1990 two cats of 11 and 21 lbs were caught. Many other waters in the area must have been stocked in the same way, though in recent years it has been possible to obtain consent to do some catfish stocking, and a number of lakes in different parts of the country have now had catfish put into them quite legally, and there are many more to follow, I feel. At least two waters have been stocked legally, with Water Authority and M.A.F.F. permission, with fingerlings from my

Baby catfish from Withy Pool in Bedfordshire about to be released into a new water with Water Authority and Ministry permission.

water, Withy Pool in Bedfordshire. These were, John Wilson's lake at Norwich, Norfolk in 1988 and Wrest Park at Silsoe, Bedfordshire in 1989. By the end of the 80's many more waters had been stocked by anglers including two lakes in Norfolk and the River Thurne system.

Catfish are predatory, and they often don't feed regularly in our 'cool' waters, which means that fishing for them is often very slow, and you may go for long periods without takes, but the long waits are well worth while when you do eventually hook one of these powerful fish and experience its remarkable fighting qualities. The contrast between the long periods of inactivity and the frantic excitement of the fight is even more pronounced than in carp and pike fishing, and you need the sort of temperament that can cope with this type of fishing—a temperament which most big fish anglers have naturally, or they wouldn't indulge in this kind of fishing.

The wels is widely distributed in Eastern Europe and in Asia, particularly in the Danube and Volga basins, though it has been introduced to some rivers and lakes in Germany, France, Spain and Holland. It is especially suited to the slow flowing reaches of the larger rivers, and to rich lakes with dense weedbeds and muddy bottoms.

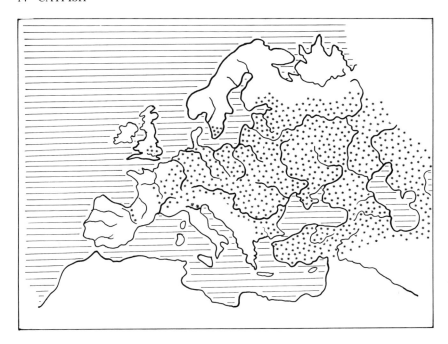

Map showing approximate distribution of *Silurus glanis.*

The body is long and almost cylindrical (scientists call it 'anguilliform' which means eel-like), and the skin does not have obvious scales. There is a big mouth with six barbels, two long ones on the upper jaw, and four short ones under the lower jaw. The hundreds of teeth are very small and are arranged in a row towards the front of the mouth on both jaws. These teeth are quite 'soft' and slope inwards towards the back of the mouth. A little in front of the throat cavity are two convex bones in the upper jaw that 'marry up' to a concave plate in the lower jaw and these are for crushing the prey prior to swallowing. Another interesting feature is the numerous short spikes on the inner edges of the gill rakers and these are used for manipulating the prey once inside the mouth. This description might sound awful to non-catfish anglers but I can assure you that it is quite safe to put your hand right down inside a cat's mouth to remove a hook—something you wouldn't do with a pike! Since the wels relies mainly on the barbels to find food, the eyes have, through evolution, become very small, which also seems to indicate that it is mainly a nocturnal feeder. The colours vary according to the habitat, but at usually brownish or grey-black with a mottled pattern along the lateral

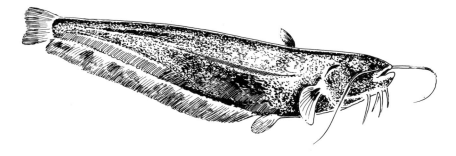

Silurus glanis.

flanks. In very clear waters the body is almost black whilst in heavily coloured waters it is a very light colour.

It is known to live for up to 60 years. 'A Report on the Catfish' by J. L. Fraser and Dr. D. J. Shillcock of the Yorkshire Water Authority states that an authentic record of one fish, taken from the River Dnieper, in Russia, was 5 metres in length and weighed 306 kg— which is well over 600 lbs! A catfish of 100 lbs will be about 6 feet in length; my 113 lb cat from Germany measured 6 ft 7 in, and it is the length of this powerful body which enables the catfish to fight so hard when hooked—in Spain they have towed our boats up river for up to three quarters of a mile!

People often describe the wels as 'ugly', but I don't really agree with this. I would prefer to think of them as strange and unusual in appearance, and they are certainly primitive looking—which is hardly surprising, as they are a very old form of fishes which has been around for many millions of years. I've known even a thirty pound carp described as 'ugly', so although the catfish is certainly not a 'pretty' fish, I think its appearance is very impressive and exciting.

They spawn from May to July, as carp do, and need a water temperature of around 20 Celsius (68 deg.F) or more, again just as the carp do, and the eggs hatch in about three days dependent on temperature. The larvae measure about 7mm in length, and already have a small barbel. After the yolk sac is absorbed they feed exclusively on plankton, later becoming more predatory and feeding on small fish. They will also eat frogs, toads, rats and insects.

The growth rate is quite fast, but depends on the water temperature to a large degree—the warmer the water, the faster the fish grow, and in ideal conditions they may reach a weight of about two pounds in two years. However, the average growth rate in the U.K. is about one pound per year. Catfish feed best in warm water, often at night, although they can be caught during daytime. In the UK they often seem to spend some days without feeding—one of the aspects of catfish which makes them hard to catch, but before feeding the fish becomes 'an active, cruising predator'. They feed very little in the winter and few are caught in water temperatures of below 50 degrees F.

Fears that because of their size they will destroy all the small fish in a water are completely unfounded, and are not borne out by facts. At Claydon Middle Lake, which is very shallow and contains many catfish, and where they have existed for 40 years, there are many thousands of small fish—so many that a landing net dipped into the margins will often produce 5 or 6 small carp, roach and bream. The catfish fill about the same place in the ecological balance of a water as pike do, and therefore are an excellent fish to have in most waters, especially those which are heavily stocked with small fish such as roach and rudd. Tring Reservoirs are further proof that catfish are not detrimental to other species where a population still exists today, some 85 years after stocking, in one of the most productive all-round fisheries in the country; big match weights and specimen fish are still a regular occurrence on Marsworth where all other species live in harmony with the wels. Water Authorities have been understandably cautious about allowing catfish to be stocked because of the spread of other 'alien' predatory fish, such as the zander, but many are allowing catfish to be stocked in enclosed waters and this seems to be the future for them in this country even though odd specimens have been caught from rivers such as the Thames in recent years.

An enormous amount of good publicity for the catfish has been undertaken by the Catfish Conservation group, which I was instrumental in founding, and many anglers and angling authorities who were previously prejudiced against this fine fish have now changed their views after hearing the true facts about them from the CCG, and reading about them in the CCG magazine, *Whiskers*, of which I am the Editor. Through the efforts of the C.C.G., the Nature Conservancy Council (advisers to M.A.F.F) agreed to view all stocking applications to ordinary full enclosed waters, favourably in the future. I strongly advise all those interested in catfish to join the CCG, and help spread the knowledge of the catfish—it was, after all, the Pike Anglers' Club which did so much to educate anglers about the true nature of pike, and to prevent so many of them from being unnecessarily killed, and the CCG is doing a similar job for catfish, except that the problem is not persecution, more so the lack of stock fish.

Catfish specialist Bob Rolph, of the old Kent Specimen Group, whose writings appeared the Autumn 1986 issue of *Whiskers*, the catfish magazine, says:

'Most of my angling friends have shown an avid interest in the species and would jump at the chance to fish for them if only there were more catfish waters. The fighting qualities of the catfish are second to none, and the sheer power of the fish when first hooked has to be felt to be believed. If one could imagine a fish with the power of a barbel, the weight and doggedness of a huge carp, and the build of an eel—then that's a catfish!

I strongly recommend club secretaries to consider this fish when planning stocking programmes. Their members would never be away from the waterside. There seems no danger of the species over-running a fishery, as in all the catfish waters I know, other species have remained very prevalent ... naturally any proposed introduction would have to be made with the full co-operation of the Water Authorities ...'

I am pleased to be able to say that since this piece was re-published some permissions have been given, and that there are now far more waters containing catfish in England than there were four years ago. However, there is still much to be done, and I urge all those who read this book and who will, by the time they have read it, have, I hope, considerable knowledge of the true facts about catfish, to do what they can to try to see that more waters in this country are stocked with this fascinating fish.

A 'Report on the Catfish' (Yorkshire Water Authority) from which I have quoted earlier, states.

'... despite several recorded introductions during the past century only one self-reproducing population is known in this country, and the species for the most part has remained confined within closed waters to which it was introduced.'

Although since this was written catfish have been shown to have bred naturally in several other English waters, amounts of small catfish have not been great, and they can certainly be introduced into enclosed waters without any danger, either to other species, or of spreading to the river systems.

Those who are frustrated by the comparatively small number of waters in this country containing catfish are well advised to try fishing for them in Continental countries, where, as I have said, they have grown much larger than they have in England, and where a wels of 100lbs, is not considered particularly large. Be warned, however, that in most cases these fish are killed when they are caught in other countries. A 'Report on the Catfish' says:

'The flesh of the wels, especially those weighing between two and four kilos, is tasty and appreciated in central Europe, especially in Hungary

It is not rare for catfish to have a deformed feeler such as this one.

and Yugoslavia. Indeed, in central Europe where there are no eels, wels replace them as a delicacy and a first quality fish.'

I have put this in my introduction, not because I advise killing catfish, on the contrary, *ALL* catfish in this country *must* be treated carefully, and returned alive to the water—but as a warning to those who fish in other countries that in most cases catfish are regarded as a food fish, and will be killed and eaten . . . just as we do with cod—and trout!

At the start of my introduction, I said that I should say that the 90's could well be the 'decade of the catfish', once English anglers discovered the excitement of fishing for, and of catching, this powerful predator. In this book I hope both to educate my readers and to interest them in the wels, and also to show how they can be caught, using normal English methods, tackle and baits: if I succeed, as I hope I will I am sure that many more anglers will come to appreciate this exciting fish as much as I do, and that more and more catfish will be caught by more anglers.

Baits

Silurus glanis locates its food by smell, or by sensing, and homing in on, vibrations. It can be caught on virtually any dead or live bait, from as small as a single maggot to a bait half the size and weight of the catfish. Generally, any *meaty* or *fishy* bait of a soft texture is best. Listed is what I have found the most successful and they are covered in approximate order of preference on UK waters.

Livebaits

Catfish are extremely sensitive to vibrations and live fish rank as their most common food. Small livebaits hooked through the top lip, or root of the tail, are usually best and here a hook with a wide gape greatly assists hooking ability; the bait must be a 'loose' fit on to the bend otherwise the possibility of self-pricking and striking through the bait is greatly reduced. Rudd and roach seem to be preferred above all other species but as far as the catfish angler is concerned they are not the most practicable as often they do not live long. Common and mirror carp, tench or crucian carp live a long time on the hook and are therefore a wise choice; they are very strong fish and survive well when forced to work continually on legered poly-ball and paternoster set-ups. Gudgeon are quite good but perch and bream do not appear to make good livebaits (although perch are an excellent deadbait).

Seafood Deadbaits

Second to livebaits are the seafood deadbaits and the sole reason for their tremendous success is their strong smell. I have often wondered which type of bait a catfish can sense from a greater distance; a tethered livebait or a piece of squid? I first used squid for catfish in the early 80's, following my success with squid boilies for carp. At the time no-one had ever tried it. I should therefore like to claim its introduction to catfishing as it has probably caught more English cats than any other bait including Britain's most notable catfish—Kevin Hampton's 39 from Tring! A

Kevin with a 30½ and a 24½, both of which picked up a piece of squid soaked in worm extract.

2 inch section of a small calamarie is usually best, and why most anglers remove the backbone is unbeknown to me; cats are quite used to hard bones in live and dead fish, so the very soft virtebrae of the squid is hardly likely to put the catfish off. As well as using it raw, I have had a lot of success soaking or cooking squid in Ace worm extract or ox blood. Make sure the lady of the house is out when cooking squid in worm extract for obvious reasons! Sea mussels, whelks and cockles have all produced 20 pound cats for me, with whelks being most effective when soaked or cooked as per the squid. Sea mussels could be a more effective bait than squid if firm ones were easily obtainable; most commonly available sea mussels are very brittle and fall apart easily. I have tried other seafood baits, including prawns, but they are not as good as the ones mentioned.

Freshwater Fish Deadbaits

Without a doubt, roach and perch make the best freshwater fish deadbaits for catfish. Foolishly, very few anglers are willing to try perch, probably because of its spiked dorsal, which is a shame because it is so good. I always pierce the swim bladder, as the fish can become a 'floater' a few hours after death, and cut the lower body between the vent and the back of the head so that more of the body juices emit thereby enabling the cats to locate the bait from a greater distance. I have had success with dead fish at varying degrees of decomposition but now always use the freshest available. My next choice, following on from roach and perch is a section of pike. A 2 inch section of a smallish pike (10–18 inches) is an excellent bait but the skin is very tough making careful hooking essential. Eel section is also very good and accounts for a large proportion of catfish captures in this country. I have also had instant success on sections of freshly killed eels that are still writhing.

Other Deadbaits

Freshwater mussels are an excellent bait when removed from the shell and used whole or just the 'foot' section. It is best to bait an area with a good quantity of free offerings but I no longer do this nowadays as a lake's valuable stock can soon be depleted. It can take years for a population of mussels to become established but only weeks for the stock to be virtually depleted if several anglers are collecting them. Bob Baldock and myself once put about 200 in a water that was hardly producing a cat at the time and within a few hours of fishing we caught several fish to 26lbs. It is still a fairly good bait when used without groundbaiting but a really excellent bait when heavily introduced. Having said all this, in most English waters I don't believe cats eat them complete with shell; pea mussels and zebra mussels, yes, but not swan mussels. If they did, you would see pieces of shell emitting from the cat's vent, or in the bottom of a sack, as you often do with the bigger continental cats.

Sea fish have also resulted in a large number of captures but mainly on the hard fished waters where cats are wary and anglers are always trying to find a new bait. The best of these is undoubtedly sprats, used whole or as a quarter. Their softness reduces casting but they are worth the extra effort and pre-baiting is definitely beneficial. Mackerel and herring, whole or in sections, catch catfish but I would only use them on the hard-fished waters. Sandeels are quite good and my friend Keith Lambert has caught many cats on them. Keith also uses day-old chicks with considerable success but one must remember to remove the feathers otherwise they float!

Meat Baits

Raw liver is an excellent bait especially when it is introduced little and often over a fairly long period. It is not unusual for a catfish to

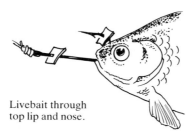

Livebait through
top lip and nose.

Two pieces of heavy rubber
band stop livebait escaping,
or working over eye and up line.

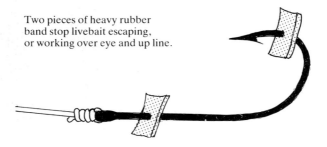

With squid, liver, sprat sections, mussels
etc., hook must stand up proud
and be mostly exposed.
If hook lies flat it will
probably be struck into
bait instead of catfish.

Pike (and eel) sections
should be hooked in similar
way to squid, liver etc.
Most of hook must be
exposed and positioned such
that it does not enter
bait upon strike.

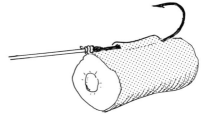

Correct Mounting of Bait.

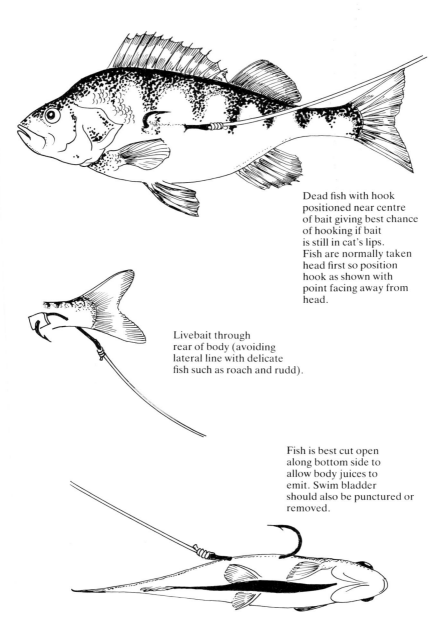

Dead fish with hook
positioned near centre
of bait giving best chance
of hooking if bait
is still in cat's lips.
Fish are normally taken
head first so position
hook as shown with
point facing away from
head.

Livebait through
rear of body (avoiding
lateral line with delicate
fish such as roach and rudd).

Fish is best cut open
along bottom side to
allow body juices to
emit. Swim bladder
should also be punctured or
removed.

Catfish expert, Des Butcher with one of his many cats.

be caught several times on liver, with ox liver being the best one. On a couple of the lakes I fish, I reckon most of the catfish population have been caught on liver more than once.

There are so many raw meat baits that will take cats that I have not tried them all so cannot comment on their catching qualities. I have seen a cat caught on bacon and I should think it would make a good bait. Luncheon meat has caught a few but again mainly on the hard fished waters—I would not use it as I am a great believer that cats prefer softer baits, if they have the choice! Bob Baldock often uses raw sausages with considerable success.

Other Baits

Lobworms are excellent but have the big disadvantage of appealing to most other species of fish. Crayfish are also quite good but are not usually easily obtainable. Paste baits made with fish meal and raw meat are sometimes very good.

Unusual Baits

I must first mention an excellent bait which I discovered in Germany and one which will undoubtedly become very much in demand in this country in the near future. It is a large leech known as a blutegal to the Germans. They are usually about 2 inches long by ½ inch wide when contracted but extend to 4–6 inches when swimming. Lightly hooked at the thicker end, they swim with abandon and send out unusual snake-like vibrations that catfish find hard to resist. Abroad, I have caught quite large fish on them and have found they also work very well here in the U.K. They can be ordered from drug stores in Germany, where they are used for human medicinal purposes, but are very expensive at about £4 each. They are tough and quite easy to keep and often can be re-used after a catfish has taken them. They can go without food for several months. It is quite amazing when you wish to get a couple out of a bucket of water; just immerse your hand, wait a few seconds and when you remove it several are automatically attached whereupon you have to 'lever' them off your skin. Rather like Humphrey Bogart coming out of an African swamp! What amazes me with the bait is that no other species of fish takes it which is a terrific advantage to the catfish angler. I have recently found a source of horse leeches which extend to 12 inches when swimming and I'm looking forward to trying them. It is definitely the unusual vibrations that account for their success and I should think that very small snakes would be the best of all; anyone know of a supply?

Another really good catfish bait used in both Eastern and Western Europe but not yet here is the maulwurfsgrille. It is a beetle-like creature about 2 inches long with wings and a hard shell that lives in the ground and has such vicious pincers on its front legs that it takes a long time to tie it onto the hook. Again, it is the unusual vibrations given off by the maulwurfsgrille that catfish find irresistible. It would catch a lot of catfish in England but I have not got round to trying it. Good luck to the first person who goes to the trouble of obtaining some—they will definitely work.

Boilies

I have caught several cats on large boilies made from raw beefburgers and on the easy catfish waters boilies have resulted in many captures. Despite this, I don't rate boilies when cats have a choice of food; we must not get misled by the 'hungry', heavily stocked waters such as Claydon and Tiddenfoot where cats are reliant on whatever is available. On the small lake at Withy Pool where I live, many cats have been caught on Maestro Oceanic boilies which are fish-meal based and flavoured with

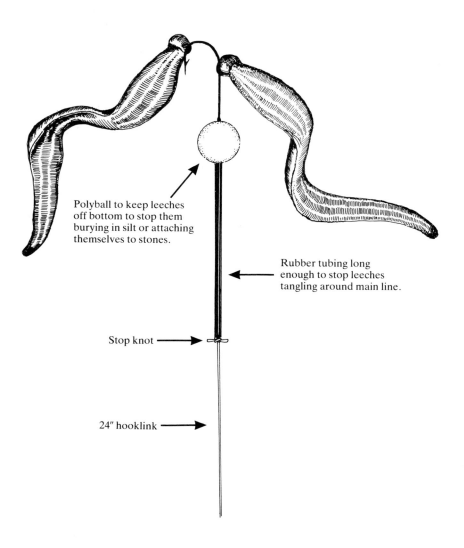

Polyball to keep leeches
off bottom to stop them
burying in silt or attaching
themselves to stones.

Rubber tubing long
enough to stop leeches
tangling around main line.

Stop knot ———►

24" hooklink ———►

Hook Arrangement for Leeches.

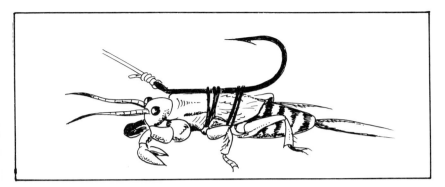

The maulwurfsgrille is an excellent bait and is best fished on a polyball set up to stop it burying or hiding on the bottom.

This Claydon double took a fancy to an extra large boilie made from raw beefburgers.

a blend of three natural fish oils. This shallow lake is one quarter of an acre yet contains about 3000 fish of a mixture of species. Competition is great and they will readily take boilies but try them on the main lake at Withy and you'll find it harder than Tring Reservoirs to catch a cat on the same boilies!

That completes my list of baits for use in the U.K. As I said at the beginning of this chapter, catfish will take anything edible but I only intended to include those that I think are the best baits.

Tackle and Tactics

The tackle needed for catfish fishing is simple, and is very similar to that used for most types of big fish in this country. If you have any carp or pike gear you are not likely to need to add to it. Any good carp rod, of the more powerful type, is right for catfish fishing, though it is worth bearing in mind that you may have to cast baits which are slightly heavier than those used for carp, so you should choose a rod with sufficient power to cast a small live or dead bait.

I suggest one of the compound taper type, with a through-action, preferably one of about 2 lbs test curve. Either fibre glass or carbon rods are ideal, as both have the strength for this type of fishing. Most of the dead or live baits used are not very large, although at times they may be quite heavy, and this should be remembered when choosing the rods you are going to use.

Either 10 ft or 11 ft rods are best—the one I use myself is the KM5, made by Simpsons of Turnford. This rod has proved to be excellent both for catching big carp and for catfish and I now use this rod exclusively for all my catfishing in the U.K.

Any good modern reel with a good clutch will do, though it should have a largish spool which will take plenty of heavy line, again the sort of reel used for carp or pike fishing will be adequate. If you are already a big fish angler you will have most of this type of tackle, but if not you will need to buy some. It is not necessary to buy the most expensive reels, though I prefer to use the latest Shimano 4000 Baitrunner Aeros, as this is a very advanced reel with advanced technical features. The Shimanos are now very popular with most big fish anglers. They are well engineered and have the clutch on the back of the reel, where it can be easily adjusted during the fight if necessary.

People seem to have very different views about the best line to use for big fish and I would therefore suggest that you use the line you are happy with and which you have proved by experience is sound and successful for big fish. If you are likely to be fishing near snags it should be a line which will stand up to abrasion, and for this it seems that many big fish anglers use Maxima or Sylcast. My own preference is for Sylcast, usually in the breaking strain range of from 11 to 15lbs. Catching big carp up to 40lbs from snaggy areas has shown this line to be more abrasion resistant than any other, so it is now the only type of line I use when fishing for catfish.

At one time I used a heavy Dacron type hooklength, Millwards Fly Line Backing, which is quite soft, and very strong, but it did not seem to make any difference as catfish are not normally line shy, though they don't like a lot of resistance on the take. For this reason, I am now using monofilament nylon tied straight to the hook usually in the 11–15lbs breaking strain class, and as I've already said I find Sylcast best for this.

Fishing a water such as Tring Reservoirs, where there is a chance of a very big catfish, I would use a heavier hook link of monofilament tied straight to the hook, perhaps of 20lbs breaking strain. This combats the wear sometimes caused on the line by the numerous small teeth of the catfish during a long fight. These teeth are not very sharp, but are quite abrasive and the occasional catfish has been lost during long fights because the teeth have worn through the line, although this mainly applies to the very big fish on the Continent, as you will see from the special chapter of catfish fishing in other countries, later in this book. The lips of the wels are nothing like as sensitive as the lips of a carp, so you are not likely to have rejection problems if you use heavy monofilament tied straight to the hook—catfish are unlikely to be able to detect this, as carp can, and reject the bait because they can feel the stiffness of the line across their lips. The catfish does not have the same type of mouth as the carp—in the wels the mouth is quite hard—in places very hard, and there are no protractile lips as the carp have. However, it should be appreciated that catfish are sensitive to resistance.

The hooks should be very large and very strong, in order to be able to cope with the huge, hard mouths of the catfish. I suggest the Partridge Z 2's, made by Partridge of Redditch, the only real UK hook maker, and one of the best in the world. Partridge have specialised in making hooks for the big fish angler, and the Z2's, have strong wire, and a very wide gape. I use size two's and 1/0's for livebaiting, and the same sizes when using deadbait. Again you should use the hooks you like and have found to be good for other types of big fish, but don't forget that the catfish has a very big mouth, some parts of which are so bony that a hook won't penetrate at all, such as the rows of teeth just inside the mouth, so you need something very big, strong and, of course, very sharp.

Most big, thick hooks are very blunt, or comparatively so, so I sharpen all mine before use very carefully. I use a file and I prefer to sharpen them to a long, tapered point. I consider this a very important aspect of catfish fishing. If you don't have very sharp hooks you will almost certainly lose fish for this reason, and as the fish you lose could be a fish of a lifetime you should take great care to have the best type of

A bunch of worms lured this Woburn Abbey double for Dave Osborne.

hook, which is well sharpened. Although this is not a very pleasant job it is essential and if you are not prepared to take the trouble to sharpen your hooks, then you must expect to lose the occasional fish. Never use a treble hook or rigs with more than one single otherwise a lost fish could die.

As far as accessories are concerned, you will need all the usual items necessary for big fish angling. Swivels are important, and they should be very strong. The best on the market are the Berkley swivels, an American type which have a very high breaking strain. It is no good using very strong line and then tying in swivels which have a breaking strain of less than the line itself. The breaking strain of Berkley swivels is marked on the packets, and as long as this is greater than the breaking strain of your line they are safe to use.

Obviously, you will need beads as well as swivels, and all the other bits and pieces needed for this type of fishing. Artery forceps to extract hooks are essential, and very long ones are sometimes needed although on the whole most catfish are hooked in the side of the mouth. For fish of over 20 lbs I do not use forceps; it is easier and quicker to put your hand and arm into the fish's mouth.

You certainly need a big landing net—bigger than normal. I recommend one with at least 48 inch arms, and these are now readily available from specialist tackle shops. Not only do you need a large net, but if possible it should be one of a special shape. The longer distance there is between the front cord and the spreader block, the better. This is important because catfish are very long, and because of their long tail they can easily slide back out of the net. You need to get the head right up to the spreader block when netting the fish, and if you have the 'long' type of net, it is less likely that the catfish will be able to slide out of it, using that very long and powerful tail. You can make the net into a 'longer' shape by keeping the front cord very tight. This pulls the net into a longer shape, but I advise looking at the net carefully before you buy it, and trying to find a net type which is longer rather than broader. Try to avoid 'micromesh' as this becomes very heavy and slow when a huge net is used. It is exceptionally important, with such a long powerful fish, to have a net of the right type and size. Obviously, if your catfish are not very large, you will have no problems with them in a normal carp type net, but if you know that the water contains big fish you would be well advised to get a very big net of the type mentioned. It often takes a long time to hook a catfish, because they go for long periods without feeding, and the last thing you want to do is to lose it at the net because you had not bothered to get a net which was big enough. The catfish is not shaped like any other British fish, except perhaps an eel, and you should be aware of this before you go fishing for it.

This leads me on to writing about retaining catfish, which is very different again because of their shape. My advice is not to retain catfish at all, if you can possibly avoid it. If you can, put them straight back. However, I admit to not always following my own advice here, and I have kept good fish, when I've caught them at night, until the morning. To me, a good photograph is an important part of fishing for big fish— after all, it's the only record you have of them once they are returned, so I will keep fish for a few hours for the sake of a picture, although I will only do this if I am absolutely sure that they will come to no harm.

Catfish can die very easily in sacks, much more easily than other big fish. After fighting to almost total exhaustion they require a lot of oxygen to recover. Another problem is that they tend to suck the soft sacking material into their huge mouths—nearly three quarters of a carp sack has been found in the mouth of a 'sacked' catfish, and this can kill the fish. Several catfish died in my own water, Withy Pool, *after* they were sacked and we have now banned the sacking of catfish to avoid further deaths. Carp sacks are not big enough, nor are they the right shape for catfish and they should be avoided. If you do use them, check the fish very frequently, to see that the catfish is the right way up and that there is no sacking in its mouth.

Bob Baldock supports a well-deserved 23-pounder from Jones Pit.

Kevin and John 'Citroen' Fairey with low doubles taken on liver from Withy Pool, Beds. The fish are very dark in colour due to the clear water.

One of the tagged catfish at Withy Pool where the growth rate of the fish in both lakes is carefully monitored.

A big weigh-sling was necessary for this lovely 30-pounder.

Kevin with Britain's rarest catfish – a 12-pounder 'albino' from Jones Pit.

A rare site indeed – a brace of 20's for Bob Baldock.

It is sometimes possible to sex a catfish. This is a female – the piece of skin alongside the vent is longer and thinner on a male.

When the water is cold, catfish tend to do very little!

Keith Lambert proudly displays a Lea Valley 20-pounder.

Kevin with a Claydon fish of $31\frac{3}{4}$ pounds.

Kevin with a $31\frac{1}{4}$-pounder taken at dusk on squid soaked in worm extract.

Matthew Schenks with a Jones Pit fish of 21¾ pounds taken on a deadbait.

The Airman Pit in Bedfordshire has provided Keith Lambert with several doubles such as this one taken on sprat section.

Martin Golder with a 34-pounder from Rackley Hills Pit at Leighton Buzzard.

Richard Tring with Claydon's biggest fish; 'The Brown One', which weighed 33 pounds at the time.

Do *not* keep the fish at all in hot shallow water, or they are very likely to die—and who wants to kill such a fine fish for the sake of a picture even if this is done by mistake?

Pike tubes are sometimes used to retain catfish, and these can work well at times. The problem with these is that they need to be pegged at both ends and naturally this can only be done in shallow water, which is often too hot for the fish. In addition, the fish cannot be seen in a pike tube and they could easily be upside down, and dying, which often happens when catfish are retained. For this reason, I am not happy with pike tubes and I will not normally use them. If you do use them, always make sure the tube is twice as big as the cat otherwise the water/oxygen exchange is not good enough for an exhausted fish.

What is really needed is for someone to 'invent' a special type of retainer for catfish. This should be tubular, but rigid so that the catfish cannot suck the material into its mouth. It would have to be portable and be able to be rigged up so that it could be thrown into deep water. Part of the retainer should be transparent, perhaps a band around the middle, so that the fish can be seen at all times, and when it is checked it would then be easy to see that the fish was the right way up and therefore safe. As soon as a 'cat' is seen to be upside down in any type of 'sack', it is undoubtedly in trouble, and it should immediately be removed from the retainer, supported in the water until it can swim upright and be released at once. This may take quite a long time, perhaps as long as an hour, but it is well worth taking this amount of trouble to ensure that this fish will survive.

Perhaps someone who is interested will come up with something of this type for keeping catfish; my suggested design is illustrated. Meanwhile, if you do keep them by any means, check them very frequently and return them if they are in any distress. I have never killed a catfish by keeping one for a few hours, and as I've said, I do it sometimes, but I am not very happy about keeping them at all and if there is any reason to suspect that I may be doing them some harm I will put them back at once, even if this means that I miss out on the photograph.

Later in the book, I shall be writing about another method of retaining catfish (the stringer), which is regularly used by anglers in other countries and one that I would not hesitate to use if I caught a really big cat in England.

A very big weighing sling is also needed, and fortunately it is possible to buy big slings of this kind from many tackle shops which cater for the specimen hunter. Two types I know of are the big slings made by ET Products, and by Kevin Nash. Catfish are hard to weigh because of their length and a sack is not suitable as they will get very badly bent up in one, so try to obtain the right type of weighing sling.

Although, as I have already said, long artery forceps may be needed

Two rigid bars (180° apart) fitted into place just before use.

See-through mesh centre section to encourage good water exchange and enable angler to inspect cat with torch at night.

Long cord of at least 5 metres

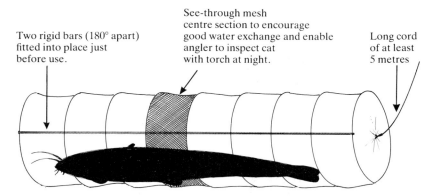

The above is my idea of the ideal catfish retainer – I do not have one like this but I have shown it in the hope that a tackle manufacturer might produce one. I have used all types of sacks, tubes, etc. including unusual ones not on the market and I am certain that the above design would be safe to use. The E.T. Pike Tube could be converted as the existing shape and materials are adequate. The centre section would need to be changed to see-through mesh and provisions for two rigid bars (which could be stiff canes) would have to be made. The rigid bars could easily be carried in the angler's rod holdall. Come on you specialist manufacturers – let's have one!

for the rare occasions when your catfish does get hooked further down than usual, and they are not easy to weigh because of their length, it should be noted that catfish are exceptionally docile once they are on the bank. As a rule, as soon as they emerge from the water, they lie quite still and rarely move at all, which makes handling them very easy. They certainly move about much less than any other species I have ever come across, although I don't know the reason for this.

Most people will be using electric or electronic bite indicators, but these should not be of the antenna type as these cause too much resistance to a taking fish. As I have already said, catfish are sensitive to resistance, and you can minimise this by using bite indicators of the Optonic or Bi-Tech Viper type, as these have less resistance.

Obviously, you will want a visual indicator on the line as well. If you are freelining, a very light indicator of the kind which 'drops off' the line is best. When link-legering deadbaits, you still need a very light indicator, but this should be on a full length 'needle' and should not drop off the line.

For livebaiting, almost any indicator will do, but a heavier type is needed because of the action of the livebait and its movement, and the livebait anyway is nearly always taken confidently by catfish. To take livebaits the catfish cannot afford to be finnicky otherwise it would rarely

Drop-off indicator
Ideal for free lining and close range fishing with deadbaits.
Use short needle, lightweight indicator with bail arm open.

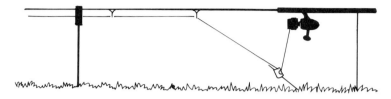

Standard indicator
Standard set-up for ordinary legering techniques.
Lightweight indicator, open bail arm, line held *lightly* in run clip.

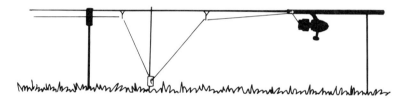

Livebaiting set-up

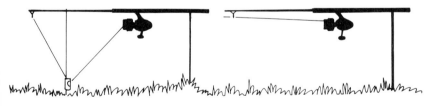

Use indicator heavy
enough to check movements of
livebait so that no false bites
occur. Carp type monkey climbers
are usually suitable.

If using Shimano Baitrunner,
use baitrunner on lightest
possible setting—no indicator
required.

catch them! I would advise using the carp-type 'monkey climber' indicator when livebaiting for catfish. Alternatively, if you are using Shimano Baitrunner reels you can dispense with the heavy indicators and adjust the Baitrunning facility to 'check' the movements of the livebaits.

When freelining in particular, the catfish will sometimes drop the bait if it feels any resistance, so this should be minimised by any method possible. Since most fishing for catfish is going to be carried out at night and in summer, the catfish are not going to be able to see the line, but they can still feel resistance, of course, so some care must be taken over this aspect of catfish tactics, especially on hard fished waters such as Claydon, where all the fish have been caught a number of times and are caught several times a season. Like any other fish, the catfish will become more wary if they are fished for, and caught a lot.

Tactics and Methods

Location, and where to fish, is obviously important and there is a difference in approaches between clear and opaque waters. When the water is clear, the fish will feed mainly when light levels are low, which means mostly at night. The normal feeding period on most catfish waters in this country appears to be between sunset, which is about an hour before dark, when the light levels start to decrease, until about two hours before it gets light. I have not found dawn to be a good time—early in the night is usually much better, before light levels start to rise.

In daytime, I would expect to find fish in deep water, or, if there are trees and snags, underneath them. Catfish need to hide in daylight, and I have often observed them under canopies of bankside trees, with their heads under the branches, and the rest of their bodies and their tails in the open water. I have been able to swim in a wet-suit under them, and to watch them whilst they lie immobile, presumably considering that they are completely hidden, because their heads are under cover. This will only occur in quiet areas, as they must have quiet. If the banks are busy with people and their noise, they are certain to seek deeper water where they can get some peace and quiet. Recently, I was able to film catfish holding-up in the daytime and this marvelous footage can be seen in the video *Cat Fever*.

For a fishing area, I would look for a shelf or shelving area as near as possible to the place where they are likely to be holding-up. Unlike carp, catfish will not feed in a hot-spot. They will often cover large areas of a lake to find the food they want, as they are a hunting-type predator. Even if they are not actually feeding or looking for food, they may sometimes be tempted to feed if the bait is fished very near to their 'holt'. In my own lake, which is 2¾ acres, when the occasional catfish has died, different baits from three different types of areas spread all round the lake have been found in the stomachs of catfish, which just goes to show how they will travel round the lake, feeding at the same time and even picking up foods such as boilies, which are certainly not their preferred type of food. Obviously, however, they do eat them, and they are sometimes caught on boilies and other baits intended for other species especially during very hot spells when food demands are high.

In opaque, or muddy, waters, I would still choose to fish at night as much as possible, although in this type of water there is likely to be more feeding by day. I would say from experience that whilst in clear waters catfish will feed at night 95 per cent of the time, in muddy waters there might be on average thirty per cent daytime feeding and only 70 per cent at night. In addition, their feeding habits are undoubtedly affected by angling pressure and if there are usually a lot of anglers on the water during daylight hours, the catfish tend to feed at night even more. On two or three occasions I have been given permission to fish small private lakes where there was little fishing, and I have always caught 'cats' immediately, and all day. Even fish of 20 and 30 pounds have been caught in the same way, so their feeding is not perhaps as naturally nocturnal as might be supposed. Perhaps it has been man's persecution of catfish over several hundred years that has made them adapt to mainly night feeding?

In these muddier waters, the catfish may be found anywhere. They are not necessarily attracted to snags and weed, although angling pressure may make them seek these areas. If there is little angling pressure you should find them in open water, especially in areas which are quiet. In this sort of water you can fish anywhere with some hope of success, and I would look for features on the bottom such as shelving areas, where the water changes from shallow to medium depths.

As I've already said, this will be mainly summer fishing—catches start to decrease as soon as early October, when the water begins to become colder. This obviously points to winter fishing for catfish being very poor. They do occasionally feed in the winter, and some have been caught, but on the whole winter fishing for catfish is so difficult that I cannot regard it as worth trying. However, as soon as the time arrives when I become bored with winter carp fishing I intend to spend a complete winter cat fishing.

Bait

My first choice of bait on a new water would have to be livebait, although I would not use this method if there are many small pike, which take the livebaits all the time. If there are a lot of pike, I would use a dead freshwater fish, and roach and rudd seem to be the best. This would be a good choice especially if you were able to bait up with the

29½ pound of pure muscle that fought for 30 minutes.

Simon Clarke looks happy with this cat caught whilst on a Catfish Conservation Group fish-in at Woburn Abbey, from the Baskin lake.

small dead fish, or pieces of them. Obviously, if you don't like using livebait at all, then deadbait fishing would be the method to choose.

My second choice would be a strong smelling bait, such a squid or liver, although again you normally need to be able to pre-bait first with this type of bait, as it is obviously a food which is not naturally found in the water. Small pieces are best, as on the whole large baits for catfish are not needed when fishing in this country (see the bait section for more detailed information on baits for catfish).

Whatever bait or method you use, you will have to put in the hours in order to be there for the time when the catfish start to feed, which, as I have already said is not at very regular intervals!

Rigs

Freeline fishing is easy, and with no attachments on the line and with the use of a light indicator, this must be a good method, as there will be the smallest amount of resistance. This method is very good for dead baits at reasonably close range, but it does not work well for long range fishing, because of possible line drag at these distances, and a greater

Running link leger

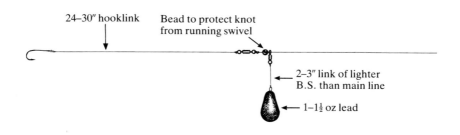

24–30″ hooklink

Bead to protect knot
from running swivel

2–3″ link of lighter
B.S. than main line

1–1½ oz lead

Livebait rig

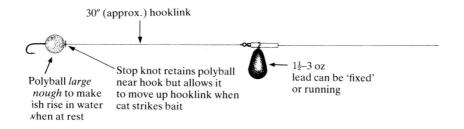

30″ (approx.) hooklink

Polyball *large
nough* to make
ish rise in water
when at rest

Stop knot retains polyball
near hook but allows it
to move up hooklink when
cat strikes bait

1½–3 oz
lead can be 'fixed'
or running

Semi-fixed lead

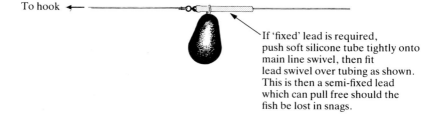

To hook

If 'fixed' lead is required,
push soft silicone tube tightly onto
main line swivel, then fit
lead swivel over tubing as shown.
This is then a semi-fixed lead
which can pull free should the
fish be lost in snags.

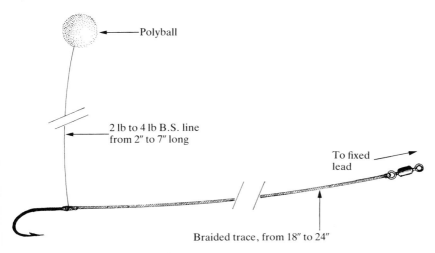

Bob Baldock's Livebait Poly Rig.

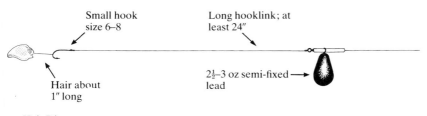

Hair Rig.

possibility of an increased risk of line 'bites' due to there being so much more line in the water.

The running link leger is a very good method for deadbaits and bait such as squid or liver. I advise having a swivel link of about two or three inches and of a lesser breaking strain than the main line. The swivel should be strong, with a large hole, and should be tied in the main line as a stop, with a bead on the line to protect the knot. A long hook link 24–30 inches, works best. Deadbaits can be fished at long range with this method, using a 1 oz to 1 ½ oz lead.

For livebaiting you will need a heavier lead, of from 1 ½ to 3 ozs dependent on size of bait and distance fished. This is normally fished directly on the line, either as a running leger, or a semi-fixed lead. If you use a polyball, which means that the bait will rise off from the bottom above the weight, then you will need a 30 inch hook link, though this does depend to a certain extent on the depth of the water, and in shallower water you may only need a hook link of 12″ to 24″.

In hard-fished waters like Claydon and Tiddenfoot it is well worth trying a hair-rigged bait, but do not use this method with a livebait, as it is bound to tangle if you do. When using a hair-rigged bait for catfish, it is best to use a long hook link and a 3oz fixed lead with a fairly small (size 6 or 8) hook, which pricks the fish much more easily than a big hook does when using the hair. I would suggest that the best length of the hair would be about an inch, although you may need to experiment with this on different waters. With catfish, the purpose of the hair rig is not to decieve the fish or to present them with softer line over the lips, but to have an exposed hook in order to encourage self hooking and lead to easier penetration. When Len Middleton and I invented the hair rig in 1980 it was to overcome the problem of carp detecting nylon line across their lips; this is not a problem with catfish as their jaws are not very sensitive.

With all these methods and rigs, it is most important to pay attention to how the bait is hooked. If the bait is on the hook, make sure the hook point, barb and 50% of the bend is not obscured, and that it does not turn into any part of the bait. Many anglers have failed to hook catfish after a take because their hook point was covered, or it turned into a hard part of the bait, so make sure that you put the baits on carefully so that the hook will easily penetrate the mouth of the catfish.

In general, methods and rigs for catfish are quite simple, and nothing too sophisticated is normally needed. Just make sure that the hook point is well exposed at all times with all methods and that there is as little resistance to taking fish as possibly, especially when using all methods except livebaits, although even here resistance may be important if the fish have been caught on a number of occasions.

Waters Where Catfish Can Be Caught

Contrary to general belief, there are now more than 50 waters in this country where catfish can be caught. Many of these are in Buckinghamshire and Bedfordshire, close to Woburn where the fish came from originally, but there are now waters containing catfish in many parts of the country.

In this chapter, I will give some detailed information on the main catfish waters and will then list some others.

Claydon Middle Lake

Near Winslow, in Buckinghamshire, is easily the best known of the waters containing catfish. It was the first club water stocked with the species, in 1951. It is a small lake, of only about 2½ acres, and is long and narrow. It is in a pleasant situation in the grounds of Claydon Park, and the big house there is open to the public, as Florence Nightingale once lived there.

The lake is shallow, only two to three feet deep, and is typical of many of the muddy bottomed Estate lakes of this type. The water is very opaque, being stirred up by the large quantities of fish in the water. The carp grow to 20lbs, and there are good bream, big zander, thousands of roach, and even golden carp to over 10lbs.

This is the easiest water in England for catfish. I estimate it now holds two thirty pounders, six 20's, and about 30 doubles, and perhaps 20 smaller catfish; the lake record for catfish is 36lbs. Night fishing is not allowed, and the lake is about half a mile's walk across fields, as the cars have to be left at the roadside.

36 catfish of up to 11lbs in weight were stocked into this lake in 1951, and there was possibly one other very large fish which was put in at the same time, as in 1953 a 27½ pounder was caught. In 1956 Bob Haynes landed Britain's first 30lb catfish, although this was accidentally foul-hooked on a spinner.

Claydon Lake can produce super catches like this 26½ and 15 pounder.

The fish grew quickly, as there was plenty of food for them and also because they were not being caught.

In the 1961/62 season, Reg Hutt, fishing for catfish, caught a fish of 33 lbs 12 ozs, which after a long campaign was eventually recognised as an official British record.

The water is fished on a season ticket only, which can be obtained from Bailiff, Jim Brennan on the bank, from Leighton Buzzard Angling Club, or from local tackle shops. There are no day tickets, and, as I have already said, no night fishing; the grounds are closed to anglers between one hour after sunset and one hour before sunrise. For a detailed account of what one can expect at Claydon see the chapter 'Golden Summer with the Neglected Giant' in *In Pursuit of Carp & Catfish*.

As Claydon Middle Lake is so heavily stocked, it is ideal for the beginner, though catching catfish from there is not much of an achievement, as it is too heavily stocked, which tends to give anglers the impression that catfish fishing is easy. This is not so in most waters, where it is normally much harder than this, with long waits for the fish to feed. Having said this, we are all grateful to L.B.A.C. for giving thousands of anglers a real chance of catching a cat over the last 40 years.

Tiddenfoot Pit, Leighton Buzzard

This water was stocked by anglers from Woburn and Claydon in the mid-60's and it is a old sandpit of about six acres with depths of up to about 10 feet. Night fishing is allowed, and there are few restrictions. This is another Leighton Buzzard Water, and is fished on the same ticket as Claydon. Tickets are not normally obtained on the bank, and must be bought in advance from leighton Buzzard Angling Club, or from local tackle shops.

There is a very good head of double figure catfish, with some 20's, and the lake record is about 29 lbs. The fish breed well and there are plenty of catfish of all sizes in this pit.

Rackley Hills Pit, Leighton Buzzard

This is a 6 acre sandpit in the town of Leighton Buzzard. Tickets from Leighton Buzzard Angling Club, and local tackle shops, season tickets only. There is a night syndicate on this water from June until October, and permission for membership must be obtained from the club committee.

The pit varies in depth from two to twelve feet, and there are a number of snags and sunken trees in the water. I would guess that there are three or four thirties, about 10 twenties and a reasonable number of doubles and singles in the pit, and they seem to breed well so there are some smaller fish.

The record for the water is about 34lbs and it is thought that much bigger fish exist.

Jones's Pit, Heath and Reach, near Leighton Buzzard

There are two lakes on this site, one of which is eight acres in size, and the other only one acre. Both are disused sandpits and lie to the west side of the A.5 trunk road.

The main lake is from two to eleven feet deep and has two islands. There are probably three or four 20's in this lake, with a reasonable number of doubles and singles. The lake record is about 26lbs and the original stock fish came from Woburn and Claydon in the early 60's. The fish breed well and baby catfish are seen every summer.

The small lake certainly contains some catfish, though it was flooded not long ago, and some of the fish may have gone into the main pit. Five years ago Bob Baldock spotted a catfish of over 30lbs, in this small pit, and he and I did hundreds of hours fishing there to try to catch it. After two summers, trying every bait and method we knew, we had to give up, having only caught a few small catfish, but the big one could still be there and would represent a big challenge to anyone who wanted to try for it. These waters are controlled by Leisure Sport Angling Club, and tickets are obtainable from them at Thorpe Park, Staines Road, Chertsey, Surrey. Tel: Chertsey 64872.

The Airman Pit, near Shefford, Bedfordshire

This lake is about three acres in size, and is alongside the A600 Hitchin to Shefford road. It is a pleasant, reed-fringed lake with depths of up to 30 feet, as it is an old clay pit. Recently, the club has filled in some of the deeper water, to create shallower areas. It is run as a carp water, and the catfish were probably put in from Tiddenfoot and have been in the water for at least 20 years. They seemed to stay small for a long time, but recently growth rates have improved, and many catfish to mid-doubles are being caught, with the lake record about 16lbs. It was rumoured that this lake produced an upper 20 some years ago but this has never been authenticated and can therefore be disregarded.

The lake is controlled by Shefford and District Angling Club, and the water is open to all on a club season ticket. Night fishing is allowed.

Arlesey Lake, Beds.

Which is in Arlesey near Hitchin, and which used to be a Hitchin Angling Club water, is an eight acre disused clay pit, now owned by David Beetham. The lake was made famous by Richard Walker, who caught huge perch from the very deep water here, and who invented the Arlesey Bomb to enable him to cast far enough to reach the perch. This is a very deep water, some of which goes up to 60feet. It contains big fish of most species, with carp to 30lbs. It is now being partly filled in to create some shallows to improve the fishing.

There have been catfish in the lake for over 20 years, though it has not been known as a catfish water. It now contains a reasonable head of catfish to over 20lbs, although the sizes and potential of this lake as a catfish water are not really known. Tickets to fish are issued by the owner on the site of Eton Bury Farm, Arlesey, or by contacting the fishery manager Robert Livock.

Withy Pool, Henlow Camp, Beds.

There are two lakes here, one of which is about 2¾ acres in size, and is an eighty year old clay pit with depths of from 2 feet to 30 feet. The lake has been landscaped and is most attractive, with many trees and bushes. There have been catfish in the lake for over 20 years, and the lake record is 18lbs. One or two much bigger fish have been seen, and there is a reasonable head of doubles and singles. The lake also contains carp to over 40 lbs, and the water record is 41 lbs.

The small lake was dug in 1987, and is only about a quarter of an acre in size. It was stocked with catfish bred naturally in the main lake of about one inch long and then raised in captivity to about 3lbs before stocking and there are now about 25 fish to 11lbs. This is a very shallow water, and ideal for catching your first catfish. There are many carp to nearly 20lbs., and tench, roach and koi carp.

As I expect you will know, I own this property and anyone interested in fishing there should apply to me at Withy Pool, Henlow Camp, Beds. SG16 6EA. Tel: 0462–816960 (Beekay Publishers). There are three caravans for fishing holidays, which are on the bank of the lake; free brochure available from Withy Pool. There is also a syndicate on the water, and at present there are some vacancies for catfish anglers. Night fishing is allowed on the small lake for those taking caravan holidays, and those renting the caravans can also fish the main lake during the day time.

These are the main catfish lakes of the country, but there are also catfish worth fishing for in the following waters, all of which are listed in every issue of the Catfish Conservation Group's colour magazine *Whiskers* and consistently brought up to date.

Woburn Park, Bedfordshire, (though fishing is not allowed in these waters at present)
Ledburn Pit, Leighton Buzzard, Beds. (Fishing not allowed at present due to gravel workings)
Workingmen's Club, Leighton Buzzard, Beds.
Lower Lake, Claydon Park, Winslow, Buckinghamshire. (London Brick Co.A.C.)
Snowberry Lake, Little Brickhill, Bedfordshire.
Vauxhall's Pit, Woburn Sands, Near Woburn, Beds.
Tingrith Pit, Beds.
Hyde Lane Lakes, Buckingham.
Church Pool, Lillingstone Dayrell, Bucks.
Blue Circle Pit, Houghton Regis, Dunstable, Beds.
The Grand Union Canal between Milton Keynes and Tring.
Tring Reservoirs—Marsworth, Startops and Wilstone, near Tring, Herts. (Day and night tickets available)
Turnford Pit, Herts (Abbey Cross Angling Society)
Stanborough Lakes, Welwyn Garden City, Herts (Day ticket water, no night fishing)
Withy Pool. Dawley, Shropshire.
Vauxhall Lake, Stanton Harcourt, near Oxford.
Corby Boating Lake, Corby, Northants.
Husborne Crawley Lake, Bedfordshire (near Woburn)

Robert Coote with a Withy Pool double that took a liking to raw liver.

A somewhat younger Peter Stone with a 12 pounder from Snowberry Lake.

Lymm Dam, Cheshire, just outside Manchester (Lymm Angling Club)
Tear Drop Lake, Milton Keynes, Bucks.
Willen Lake, Milton Keynes, Bucks.
River Ouzel, between Milton Keynes and Leighton Buzzard.
Stockgrove Park Lake, near Great Brickhill, Bedford.
Sale Marina, Gt. Manchester.
John Wilson's Lake, Norwich, Norfolk. (Private syndicate)
Barton Broads, Humberside.
South Ockendon Carp Fishery, Essex. (Day ticket water, night fishing
    allowed)
Lakemore, Cheshire.
Upper River Thurne, Norfolk.
Homersfield Lake, near Wortwell, Suffolk. (Syndicate water)
Shatterford Lakes, near Kidderminster, Hereford and Worcester. (Catfish
    to 20lbs., night fishing allowed).
Sandpiper Pit, near Newark on Trent, Notts. (Neville Fickling's syndicate
    water)

    There are several other private waters which hold a few catfish, but
details cannot be listed of these as the fishing is private. There are also

many other waters that have been stocked in the last five years with fingerlings that are not worth fishing at present.

All these waters hold some catfish, although sometimes there are not many in the waters. Further information on fishing any of these waters may be obtained from the Catfish Conservation Group, and back issues of *Whiskers* contain articles on some of these waters. If you want a real challenge, where you have a chance of catching a record fish, although the fishing will be very hard, I suggest that you try:

Marsworth, Startops and Wilstone, the huge reservoirs at Tring (I might see you there!)
Vauxhall A.C.'s Pit at Woburn Sands
Hyde Lane Lakes at Buckingham
Lymm Dam, Cheshire
Homersfield Lake, Suffolk.

Stocking and The Future

As catfish are not indigenous to this country, it is not always easy to obtain permission to stock them. Because of the rapid spread of other predatory fish which have been introduced, such as zander, the Water Authorities have been very wary of giving permission because they fear that the wels will spread to the river systems. Whilst I can understand this, I certainly don't agree with it. In Continental waters all over Europe and Asia, the rivers contain many huge catfish, where they do no harm at all, fulfilling the role of just another predator. These rivers in Europe and Asia are full of fish of many species with millions of small fish. Most of the species, such as carp and barbel, grow to sizes much greater than they do in this country and you can catch fish all sizes continually in these river systems, even where the catfish grow to over 200 lbs.

In addition, the catfish does not spread as widely, nor does it breed as rapidly as other predators such as pike. We all know of plenty of waters where there are too many small pike, but this simply doesn't occur with catfish, as they do not produce such large numbers when they breed.

I would like to see the catfish much more widely distributed, and I'm sure that in some of the bigger rivers they would grow to a large size. In spite of my views on this however, I don't wish to encourage the un-restricted stocking of catfish whilst this is not permitted. I would like to see more enclosed waters containing this fish, as in this way they would not be able to enter the river systems and cause concern to those who don't think that we should introduce another predator.

At present, stocking with catfish requires not only the written permission of the Water Authority, now the National Rivers Authority, but consent from the Ministry of Agriculture, Fisheries and Food (MAFF) as well. The MAFF will always consult the Nature Conservancy, but all these bodies may well look favourably on stocking with catfish in waters which have no outlet to a river system, as long as these waters are not an SSSI (Site of Special Scientific Interest). Many pits of different kinds, and some other waters that are not stream fed and there is no outlet, and with these there is no danger of the catfish being able to get into the rivers. They cannot spread, therefore, and will remain in the enclosed

Conclusive proof that catfish can live in harmony with other specimens without decimating stocks. Catfish have been present in considerable numbers in Claydon Lake for 30 years, yet this bag of bream and roach was caught by Dickie Carr whilst fishing alongside Bob Baldock and Kevin Maddocks who both caught catfish at the same time.

water into which they are stocked. It is unlikely that anglers will be tempted to transfer them illegally to rivers, because this is normally only done when the angler concerned thinks that he will have a good change of catching the fish again, and this is not likely in a river. For this reason, stocking into enclosed still waters is 'safe', and permission has been given on a number of occasions. I would expect that in future years permits would be easier to obtain, now that the Catfish Conservation Group has shown without doubt that catfish do not decimate fish stocks even in very small lakes, such as Claydon Middle Lake.

It looks as though there is a good future in this country for the spread of catfish stocking to enclosed still waters, though the small fish have a poor survival rate during the first winter,especially if the winter is a cold one. I would like to encourage more Water Authorities to allow people to stock with catfish; as I have already said, they have been in Claydon for nearly 40 years, yet the water is packed with small fish. In a recent feature by *Angler's Mail*, huge nets of small roach, carp and bream were caught, and recorded on camera, at Claydon Middle Lake at the same time as catfish anglers caught large catfish. The bulging nets of small fish were photographed and published in *Angler's Mail* along with several very big catfish. This proved quite conclusively that the catfish, even when present in large numbers as they are in Claydon, the most heavily stocked catfish water in this country, do no harm to fish stocks and cannot 'ruin' the water, as some anglers with little knowledge of these fish have maintained. I would be happy to take any of these people to Claydon and let them catch the thousands of fish of several species which exist there to show them that the catfish have not damaged the stocks of other fish in any way.

I hope that more fish farmers will stock, and breed, catfish in future, so that they become more readily available to clubs and individuals for stocking purposes and so that this fine fish will soon become more widespread in the country. At the moment the future of catfish becoming much more common is in the hands of our fish farmers.

Without the fish farmers, that other popular non-indigenous fish, the carp, would never have been so widespread in Britain. The CCG has shown by its research and enquiries into this subject that there are now many clubs who want catfish, and that if they could obtain them more easily from fish farmers they would certainly stock enclosed waters with them, for the benefit of their members.

There are one or two fish farms which do now have some catfish, and I am sure that once a breeding pattern can be established for them, that they will become much more widely available. I certainly hope so, for these powerful fish will provide much more sport for anglers in the future.

Don't forget — discarded line kills birds and other wild animals

The Catfish Conservation Group was founded on November 20th 1983, when six catfish anglers met at John Golder's house in Leighton Buzzard. The founders were John Golder, Bob Baldock, Glyn Owen and myself.

At a second meeting on January 7th, 1984, Peter Frost was asked to be Chairman, and the aims of the group were formed. As Chairman of the Carp Anglers' Association, and a Committee member of the British Carp Study Group, I had had considerable experience of one-species angling organisations, and I was sure that it was time for a Catfish Group. We included the word 'conservation' because one of our main aims was to look after the fish in waters it already existed, and to encourage the development of more waters for those who wished to fish for catfish.

We realised at the time that it would be very hard work, as there were comparatively few anglers who could be called catfish specialists, with only just a few more who were interested in catfish in any way.

We agreed that a good quality magazine was essential, and I offered to edit this, and I had already some experience as Assistant Editor of 'The Carp Catcher' the magazine of the Carp Anglers' Association. Obviously, we realised that we should have very few members at first, and that we would all have to contribute to the first magazine. We decided to call the magazine *Whiskers*, for obvious reasons, and the first issue appeared in the spring of 1984.

By then, well known big fish angler Peter Frost, from Dunstable, was Chairman, as I have already said; Glyn Owen was General Secretary: Bob Baldock was 'Lord High Everything Else' (Membership Secretary/Treasurer/Records Officer and John Golder a Committee member, with myself as the magazine Editor. We managed to get a world famous big fish angler, Jan Eggers from Holland, to be our International Representative, which was useful as he writes in angling magazines in several countries, and in more than one language.

The aims of the CCG are published in each magazine, and are as follows:-

1. To promote the conservation of existing catfish stocks and to recommend correct angling methods, treatment and careful handling of the species.
2. To encourage fish farmers to breed the European Catfish (wels) for the purpose of stocking English waters and to assist them wherever possible.
3. To negotiate, whenever necessary with Water Authorities for consent to stock with catfish.
4. To encourage fisher owners and managers to stock with wels, and to assist them in every possible legal way.
5. To prove, to whoever it might be necessary, that the presence of the wels does not significantly influence the stocks of other more popular species.
6. To compile as much literature as possible regarding the life history of the wels, and make this available to fish farmers.
7. To encourage more anglers to become interested in the wels, and to develop the CCG into an international organisation for friendship and co-operation between all catfish anglers.

The inaugural meeting of the CCG was held on 5th May 1984, and was well attended. It took place at Little Brickhill Community Centre, Little Brickhill, Milton Keynes, Bucks, and there were talks by leading catfish anglers, catfish slide shows, and many other attractions for those interested in catfish, and this was the first meeting of its kind held anywhere in the world.

The Group soon reached 100 members, with many joining on the door at the first meeting, and since then it has grown to nearly 200 members. Material permitting, the first-class colour magazine is published every six months, and is sent free to members and is sold to others, through some tackle shops and Beekay Publishers. Material is always short for the magazine so if you have any news items, pictures or articles the C.C.G. would be pleased to consider publishing them.

Meetings now take place annually in Oxford and there have often been over 100 members present to listen to talks and to watch films and slides of catfish and their captures.

Membership is open to all, even if they have never seen a catfish, and anyone, of any age, sex or nationality may join. There are no formalities or membership qualifications—pay your dues and you are a full member. at present membership costs £6 a year, plus £2 entry fee. The present Secretary is John Deverell of 136 Conistone Way, Blundell Street, London. N79DE. If you write to him and send your membership fee he will send you a copy of the magazine. There is also a finely designed metal badge which can be bought for a low cost as well as car stickers, cloth badges, etc. Back issues of *Whiskers* can also be obtained.

Members are encouraged to try to get fish farmers to stock and breed the wels, and also to try to persuade club and fishery managers to buy the fish and to stock their enclosed fisheries with them.

In the six years since its formation the CCG has done a lot to 'educate' the average angler about the catfish, and has successfully negotiated stocking permits with a number of Water Authorities. They have held meetings with Water Authorities, MAFF officials, and the Nature Conservancy and have been able to gain a favourable response in most cases from the Authorities who are in a position to control the stocking of waters in this country.

Through their magazine, and through publicity in the angling weeklies and monthlies they have been able to get many more anglers interested in the catfish, and to make them see that these fascinating powerful fish are not some alien monster but are a welcome addition to some of the enclosed waters in England.

The CCG is an independent and informal non-political organisation, although it is affiliated to the National Association of Specialist Anglers.

More members are need for the CCG and I strongly urge all those who read this book to join. As Magazine Editor I need stories, articles, good quality transparencies and black and white photographs for publication and these can be sent when you join. All pictures will be returned.

The Catfish Conservation Group can only be good news for anglers and for those interested in this large and powerful fish, now so well established in England, and I expect the organisation to go from strength to strength and to gain many more new members in the years to come. The C.C.G. needs your help so please join now.

Part 2

Catfish on the Continent

Introduction

It's not surprising when one looks abroad for good quality catfishing if you consider what England has to offer at the moment. Despite a great deal of effort by us devotees, to date (October 1990) there still has not been a 40lb catfish caught intentionally in this country. Granted there has been fish of 43½ in 1970 and 42¾ in 1990 but both of these captures were by accident whilst fishing for pike and carp and as far as achievements go these *captures* represent nothing. However, news of the *existence* of any 40 pounder in England is of course good news. The largest catfish captured in the U.K. that deserves merit is of course Kevin Hampton's 39 pounder from Tring—he had spent thousands of hours at Tring and of course, he was in pursuit of the fish he caught. When you think of the effort that Kevin Hampton and people like my friends and I have put into trying to catch a really big cat it's quite natural to look at what the Continent has to offer.

A catfish of more than 100 pounds is a very large fish but it's hard to visualise the largest authenticated specimen—a fish taken (commercially) from the River Dnieper in Russia measuring 5 metres (more than 16 feet) and weighing an incredible 306 kilos (673 pounds). In freshwater, this weight is only surpassed by such fish as the white sturgeon *Huso huso*, which may attain a weight of 1,000 kilos (2200 pounds) but this is not regarded as a true freshwater fish as much of its life is spent in saltwater.

Silurus glanis of more than 100 pounds have always been common in Eastern Europe and in the last 20–30 years are now becoming more common in Western Europe (Spain and France). In this section of the book the following chapters more than adequately cover Western Europe so I will include here a little information on Eastern Europe which the reader might find interesting.

Romania

I should have been in a position to write a complete chapter on catfishing in Romania but our planned trip in August 1990 was cancelled due to an outbreak of cholera on the Danube Delta.

It is the mighty River Danube that boasts *Silurus glanis*, commonly known as 'sheatfish', to more than 300 pounds. The northern part of the Danube Delta where it runs into the Black Sea is also the border line with Russia but it is on the Romanian side that most of the big cats are taken. The most common method practiced by locals is of course, not rod and line. As in most Eastern European countries the catfish is a valuable food fish and the majority are caught by the setting of long-lines, other 'lines' baited and fixed to trees or by netsman. One of the largest sheatfish caught on rod and line was from the Georghes Arm section of the Delta by Wolfgang Krischke in late October 1983. The fish took 3½ hours to subdue, weighed 96.5 kilos (212 pounds) and measured 227 cm (7½ feet).

If you fancy a trip to Romania in search of catfish I suggest that you contact Romania Holidays at 54, Pembroke Road, London. W8 6NX.

Russia

I hope to visit Russia for 'ssum', in the summer of 1991. A German tour company, Beluga Tours, arranges fishing trips to the Volga Delta where this huge river runs into the Caspian Sea. As previously mentioned, the largest Russian catfish on record is a 673 pound fish from the Dnieper which eventually runs into the Black Sea.

My friend Jurgen Paul, from Frankfurt, fished the Volga Delta in July 1990 and his party of eleven anglers caught more than 200 ssum! Fish in the 30–50 pounds bracket are very common and although they only managed to catch catfish to a little over 100 pounds they lost some bigger ones.

Other notable Russian fish on record are the 256 kilos (564 pounds) specimen from the Desna at Chernigou, and a 162 kilos (356 pounds) ssum from the Volga near the Seroglazinskaya stamitsa. It is also recorded that in the Dnieper, near Kremenchug, catfish weighing 200 kilos (440 pounds) are not a rarity in the Syr-Darya and the Chu.

Very few English anglers have fished in Russia but this will of course change dramatically over the next few years now that World relations are greatly improving.

Eastern Germany

There is little information available on *Silurus glanis* from this country but again this is likely to change in the near future now that the two Germany's are one. The catfish is widespread and one of the largest caught on rod and line is a fish of 73 kilos (160 pounds) caught

Part of the collosal catch of ssum made by Jürgen Paul's party at the Volga Delta in July 1990. The fish shown here weighed approximately 90, 60 and 50 pounds and all were taken on fillets of fish.

Lubos Murdock and his friend Martin Dolan admire the 202 pound catfish that took Lubos' 6 inch spoon. The sumec was eventually boated by 73 year old Rudolf Stritzko and measured 7½ feet in length. Examination of the bones showed this catfish to be 70 years old. *Photograph courtesy of Jan Eggers.*

by Hartmut Kitscha from Sanitz. Specimens to more than 200 pounds have been caught commercially.

Austria

The main fishery in Austria that produces 'welse' on a regular basis is the huge Ossiacher See at Karnten. The biggest Austrian welse came from the Ossiacher and weighed over 150 pounds but the 'official' record for the lake is 119 pounds. Two other big Austrian fish both came from the River Danube, and weighed 53 kilos (116 pounds) and 51 kilos (112 pounds). For information on the Ossiacher See write to: Thomas Weber, Kreuzwirt, A-9552, Steindorf am Ossiacher See, Karnten, Austria.

Czchoslavakia

There are huge catfish in Czchoslavakia and the biggest recorded on rod and line is 242 pounds which was caught in 1945 at Nitra bei Mlynarce. In 1983 a 202 pounder was caught from the Dyje/Vranov system on a spinner.

The biggest reported elsewhere was a 136 pounder from the River Danube in 1961. Another good place is the Vrane Dan, near Prague, and this produces many 'sumec' to 125 pounds.

The wels is known as the sumec in Czchoslavakia, and the open season is from July 1st to December 31st. Over 2,000 sumec a year are caught and recorded, averaging about 15lbs each. Night fishing is not allowed in Czchoslavakia and was a problem when I fished the Vranov dam, as the fish were obviously not feeding in the daytime when we were there. Sumec are of course caught in the daytime but it is a long way to go to in the 'hope' that they might not have switched to night feeding!

No one knows how big the sumec are in the River Dyje/Vranov Dam. The old man, Rudolf Stritzko, a local expert, told us stories and showed us the places where huge individual catfish live. They have lived there so long, all of his life in fact, and have been hooked and lost so many times that they have been given names and have gained a lot of respect. We stopped on a road bridge once and he pointed to a spot where 'The Professor' lives. I asked him how big, he said he'd seen it several times and it was at least five metres long. He was not the sort of person to exaggerate, having caught more big sumec in Czchoslavakia than any other man, and there can be no doubt that catfish to at least 500 pounds live at this place. We shall probably never know, as Rudolf assured us that they were impossible to land on rod and line and commercial fishing is not allowed in this area.

Hungary

The best wels river in Hungary is the River Raab, which is in the north west of the country. The record fish for this river, which is about 150 miles long, is 133 pounds, and fish of 80–100lbs are very common.

There are some very big catfish in the large Hungarian lakes, and there are records of fish of 168 pounds from the Poganger Sea in 1985, and 161 pounds from the Funfkirchner Sea in the same year. Catfish up to 136 pounds have also been reported from Harmas Koros.

Sweden

There are catfish in Sweden, mainly in the south of latitude 60N and the record fish weighed 132lbs, which was caught on a spinner from the River Eman, in 1981.

Finland

There are catfish in the south of Finland, especially in the province of Karelia, on the Russian border. Lakes Lodoga, Il'men, and Orega also contain them, although they are not common.

Yugoslavia

There are very big catfish in Yugoslavia, and one of the best places is the huge Vransko Lake. This is between Split and Zander, on the Adriatic coast. The record for this lake is 240 pounds, and catfish between 10 and 30 pounds are very common. This lake is 12 miles long and about 4½ miles wide. There are obviously catfish in Yugoslavian rivers, but information is hard to come by.

Switzerland

There are some very big wels in the Swiss lakes, and I have records of one caught by a Swiss lady angler of 150lbs, and the Murtensee has produced fish of 185 pounds, the official Swiss record, and 182 pounds. Another good lake is the Bielersee, and fish up to 130 pounds have been reported from this lake. Both Bielersee and Murtensee regularly produce catfish between 50 and 100 pounds.

Holland

There are 'meerval' in at least two lakes in Holland, one of which, the Westemider lake near Amsterdam airport, contains quite a number.

Kaj Jonsson with a 54 pound wels from the River Eman in Sweden.

There are also some in the Ijsellmeer and in 1940 wels of up to 5½ feet long were caught from the Braasemer Lake near Aalsmeer.

At one time the Dutch fishing authorities planned to introduce the wels throughout Holland and a large rearing programme was set up. Unfortunately, the scheme ran out of money and the huge quantity of young fish were sold to Germany!

Like Belgium, where only one or two waters contain a very small number of catfish, the Netherlands is not worth considering if you are in search of some good catfishing.

Tackle and Tactics

In some cases, rather different methods, tackle and tactics are needed for catfish fishing in Continental countries, and in this chapter I shall do my best to show the difference. Otherwise, the same tackle and tactics should be used as those listed in Part One.

Rods

For fishing in other European countries, two types of rods must be considered, as quite a bit of the fishing, and often the best, is from boats where you need different rods from those used for bank fishing.

If you are just going to a European country for a 'one-off' trip, and fishing from the bank of a river or lake for catfish, you can get away with your normal carp tackle, always remembering that you will need quite powerful carp rods, used with heavy lines. However, if you intend to go catfishing on the continent on a number of occasions you will certainly need special tackle to be sure of landing some of the huge fish which live in the Continental rivers.

For bank fishing, you will need something much more powerful than the average carp rod, as you will have to cast 2–6oz leads, with a leavy live of dead bait as well. I recommend a through-action carbon rod of at least 3 lbs. test curve. The best I know of this type is sold by Simpsons of Turnford, and is known as the Simpsons Continental Catfish Rod. It is based on their Specialist Pike Rod, cut down to give added power, and is 11 feet in length. This is an ideal length for a catfish rod, although a 10 footer is likely to be just as good. This rod will cast those heavy weights and large baits with no difficulty and will be powerful enough for the very big river catfish found in France, Germany, Spain and other countries.

For boat fishing, you obviously need a shorter rod, so a rod of the sea boat type is best. I am now using a 9 foot rod, as I have found this to be the best type of rod for boat use. Mine is the Browning Rod Craft 27 (2.7 metres) which is recommended for casting weights of 300 to 500 grammes, which means it is a very powerful rod that will cast a weight of at least one pound.

I have now come to the conclusion that the rods we used when we first went to these big rivers were not powerful enough, as we often had to play the fish for one to two hours, and the catfish was always exhausted at the end of this and took a long time to recover. With rods as powerful as this even catfish of up to 70 lbs or so will usually be landed in about 15 minutes, and will not be damaged during a too long fight. My good friend Bob Baldock, who often goes with me, uses a lighter version of the same rod—the Browning Orion 27, which is the same length but is not as powerful. Bob also used this rod for bank fishing and both models are made of fibre glass composite and are inexpensive. Don't forget that you could hook fish of 8 or 9 feet in length and 200 lbs. in weight, so it is better to err on the side of a more powerful rod, than end up using something with which you might not be able to control the bigger fish, or which may allow them to fight for too long. The only disadvantage of these powerful rods is that you get less fun out of a 20 or 30 pounder and the fight can be over in three or four minutes.

Reels

You will obviously need a big reel, with the capacity to hold at least 200 metres of 30 lb. breaking strain line. In my opinion, the best is the Shimano Baitrunner 4500. This is a big, heavy duty reel which holds a lot of line, and the Baitrunner facility of this reel is so important that I would not now want to be without it. If you are not familiar with this, it is a device that enables the spool to turn even when the bail arm is closed, so that you can use this without an indicator of any kind. When you get a take, the fish will spin the spool under a pre-set tension as it swims off, and give you plenty of time to strike. I strongly advise fishing in this way for catfish, instead of using the clutch.

This is particularly important in rivers with a strong current, and when using a livebait.

Line

For 99% of Continental catfish, I use Sylcast Blue of at least 26 lbs. breaking strain, for the main line, with a hook link of 31 lb breaking strain. The only time I will use a lighter main line is when fishing a snag free lake. Catfish are not line shy, especially as very few of them where you will be fishing have ever been hooked, so it doesn't matter how heavy your hook link is, and there is no need for the line to be any lighter than this. Buy a bulk spool of 1000 metres, so you will be able to have as long an amount as you like on your reel.

Although I said that with a powerful boat rod of the type I recommend you should be able to land most fish in a quarter of an hour, this cannot be guaranteed, and you make taken an hour even with this heavy tackle; you most have a strong hook link which will stand up to wear from the cat's teeth during a long fight, or will resist the many snags you are sure to encounter in these big rivers. Hooks must also be big, strong and thick in the wire. I use Partridge and Mustad O'Shaunessey's, preferably those made of stainless steel. I would not use anything smaller than 4/0's for any type of fish bait, live or dead, and I use 6/0's or 7/0's most of the time, and have used them up to size 12/0. With the immense mouths of these fish it is important that you get a good hook hold, and only a big, powerful hook will give this.

Make sure, too, that you use hooks with a wide gapes, and I advise avoiding the narrow gape type. They should also have short shanks, as hooks of this kind will stand up to far more pressure. Although this is a personal preference, I like my big catfish hooks to be offset, not straight, and if I do get straight ones, I bend them with pliers. These are far more likely to penetrate, in my opinion, and I was interested to find,when talking to John Wilson recently, that he had come to the same conclusion independently, and that he only used offset hooks when fishing for the very big fish. Obviously, hooks are vitally important in all forms of angling, but I would suggest that they are even more important than usual in catfish fishing. This is mainly because the fish are so large, with such big mouths, that you cannot afford to lose them once hooked. In addition, on many waters catfish fishing is quite hard and takes are not very frequent, so you need to ensure that when you do get a take, then you don't lose the fish because your hook was inadequate, or was not suitable for the job in hand. The use of such big hooks is foreign to English freshwater anglers, but for those who are going to try for Continental catfish, it is essential that they should start to think in a different way, realising that these fish are so much bigger than anything that we can encounter in the rivers of this country, and that fishing for them successfully requires the use of the sort of tackle which we should regard over here as suitable only for sea fishing . . . and this particularly applies to hooks.

With regard to knots, I use the same as in England (twice through the eye and four turns around the main line), except that I always tie an overhand knot in the end of the line first in case the knot should slip or settle during a long fight.

As far as other tackle items are concerned, don't forget that very big landing nets will be needed, with 5 foot arms a minimum, because of the great length of these fish. Fortunately, these can now be obtained from many tackle shops which cater for the big fish angler and can often be made for you if you can't get them 'across the counter'. The ones we use are especially made for us by Simpsons of Turnford, and have six foot arms. The weighing sling must also be very large, but the standard ET weighing sling will be big enough for catfish of up to 70 lbs—if you want anything bigger than this, contact ET Products, or Keven Nash Tackle, and they will make them specially for you, as they have done for us.

Although you may not like the idea, a gaff is essential, specially if you are boat fishing one of the big Continental rivers. In a very strong current flow there are times when a big catfish simply cannot be brought near enough to the boat to be landed at all either in a landing net, or by hand, and the fish might have to be gaffed. If you don't have one, you could lose a 200 lbs catfish—the fish of a lifetime—without one and most Continental anglers will use one anyway, whether you do so or not.

Catfish can be gaffed safely and successfully without damaging them, and the fish can be returned alive without any problems. To help you to achieve this, make sure your gaff is made of thin wire, preferably three sixteenth of an inch in diameter or less, and has a very wide gape of at least 3 inches.

The fish should be gaffed underneath the jaw in the centre, making sure that the point comes out through the inside of the lower jaw and towards you, so that it does not go into the upper jaw as well. The hole made will not end up by doing much more damage than the big hook you are using, and the fish swim away happily after being released. Make sure that you don't attempt to gaff the fish until it is completely exhausted and on the surface, and that you perform the operation confidently and carefully. Needless to say, I only recommend this for very large fish, mainly when boat fishing and in cases where it is impossible to use a landing net, or to lift the fish out by hand.

Tactics

Obviously most of the tactics and methods to be used for Continental catfish are similar to those described in Part One of this book, but there are some differences, which I will describe here.

When bank fishing, remember that takes from this big, active predator can be very violent, so make sure that you use strong rod rests, and that they are put very well into the ground, and not lightly, as most English anglers tend to do. Often there is a lot of tension on the rod and when there is a lot of flow and debri spring-loaded rod clamps are very useful.

Boat fishing gives you a tremendous advantage on the bigger rivers, some of which may be 500 or 600 yards wide. This means that there are big areas which can only be fished from a boat. In addition, these big rivers have stronger currents than we are used to in this country,

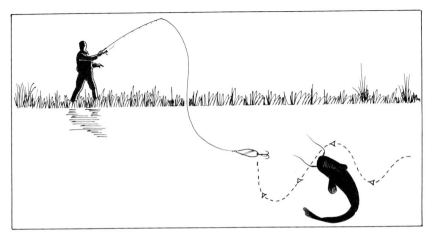

Typical Spinning Method.

and they carry great quantities of weed and rubbish which foul the line and which sometimes makes bank fishing almost impossible. Huge tree trunks and branches are brought down the rivers by floods, and these often sink, causing snags. You will be able to fish much more effectively from the boat on the larger rivers. The boats have no effect on the fish, as they do not frighten the catfish in any way. On many occasions in Spain we have had catfish knock very hard against the boat, and they will swim close to and right under the boat. We used to laugh at stories of big siluro 'attacking' the boat until it happened to us! I don't know why, but these cats often give the boat a good slap with their tails and they often lay-up underneath the boat.

It is well worth taking the trouble to take your own boat, if you know you are going to fish one of the big rivers, and if you don't have one, and intend to buy one specially, I would suggest a stable, flat bottomed boat of about twelve feet in length. I am using a fibre glass boat, which can be towed on a trailer, but a flat-bottomed craft would be better.

The boat should be anchored at both ends for stability, and should be facing the current. *Never* use anchor chains, as these can foul the line, and lose you fish, but use thin nylon rope. Don't use a conventional anchor either; all you need is a big rock tied to the end of the rope. Make sure that this goes straight down below the boat as you don't want the anchor rope to go off at an angle, when there will be more likelihood of a hooked fish going round it. The heavy Sylcast you will be using won't break if it does go round the rope whilst you are playing a fish, but a chain will certainly cut the line.

A small keepnet will be needed to hang over the side of the boat to retain spare baits. The siluro tend to grab hold of it now and again so the metal ones with spring lids are ideal and can be purchased in Spain or France.

As a hooked fish nearly always ends up downstream of the boat, bring in one of the 'anchors' as soon as a fish is hooked. The angler with the hooked fish should then obviously be sitting at the opposite end from the anchor. If I am fishing on my own I only use one anchor.

You will only need to swing the bait out a short distance, and I always cast one bait upstream with a heavier lead to hold bottom, usually 6oz and then cast a bait with a lighter weight downstream. We have our boats converted with fixed brackets, so that Optonics can be fitted directly to the boat as well as rear rod clamps which help combat the very violent takes I have mentioned earlier. The rod does need to be fixed in the boat, just as it is on the bank.

As soon as a fish is hooked, get the other person in the boat to take the other rods in first, with the one nearest the hooked fish a priority, and then take in the anchor as described above. One of the problems if often that even a very big fish will at first be wound straight in to the boat, as they have never been hooked before, so they simply don't know what is happening to them, and you think that you have only hooked a small fish. Then they start to fight violently very close to the boat, which is dangerous, so I try to get them to fight harder as far away from the boat as possible, so that they are tired by the time they come close.

If the fish goes under the boat, there is usually no problem with the anchor rope, as you can swing the rod round the boat and play out the fish downstream of the anchor. As I have said, there are some big snags in these huge rivers, and if the fish does get snagged, release the other anchor and pull the boat over the fish by using the rod and line. Once you are directly above the snag, the fish can usually be freed without too much difficulty. This is another reason for using very heavy line, and there is no reason why it shouldn't be over 30lbs. breaking strain if you are likely to encounter the conditions mentioned above—that is, big fish on a big, fast flowing river full of sunken tree branches, or very heavy weed.

If there is a very strong flow on the river, the landing net can be a big problem, as it will be large and difficult to control in the current. Make sure that you choose a net with a very big mesh which will help to alleviate this problem—I am currently getting a net specially made with a four inch mesh. I have sometimes found it necessary to handline a fish the last few feet to the boat to enable it to be netted successfully, and if you are careful it is not hard to do this with a very tired fish, even if it is big, bearing in mind the very heavy line you will be using.

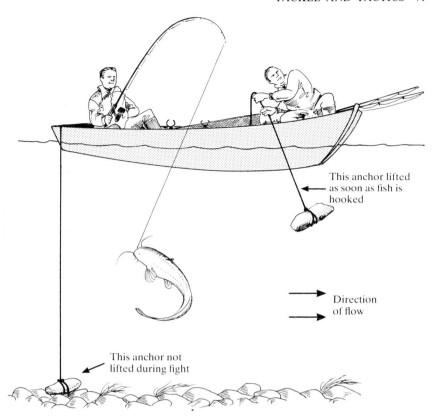

This anchor lifted as soon as fish is hooked

Direction of flow

This anchor not lifted during fight

Boat Fishing Arrangement on Rivers.

It is probably best to put the rod down if you have to do this, first making sure that the line will run out from the spool if the fish does make a last dash for freedom, and you have to let go of the line. An alternative to netting or gaffing is to land the fish by hand. Most German anglers do this and I first learnt exactly how it is done from my good friend Peter Ploetz from Nurnburg. Bring the beaten fish to the margins and kneel down, at which point you can opt for laying the rod on the ground, giving it to someone else of keeping hold of it. Pull the fish to within arm's reach and put the thumb of your free hand into the cat's mouth. At the same time, clench your hand and bring it hard up under the chin as if squeezing the thumb and top of forefinger together. Once together grip tightly and the cat cannot escape because its small

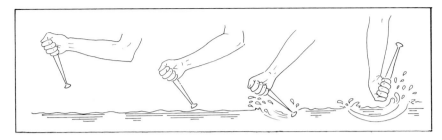

The Butchelo
This wooden tool is widely used throughout Eastern Europe to attract catfish. It imitates catfish feeding on small fish near the surface and is very effective.

teeth give good grip to the thumb. At this stage, if it is over 30 pounds you will need to insert the other hand also. Once the cat's head is out of the water a few inches it has no strength at all to pull back. This is an excellent way of landing a cat from bank or boat. Most English anglers intending to fish abroad can practice on our smaller fish first. A glove is useful for the squeamish!

Keeping Catfish on a Stringer

This is a method which is foreign to the English angler, but is widely used by fishermen in other countries. When I first saw it I disliked the idea, but now I use it for big catfish and it is much safer for the fish than to keep them in a sack of pike tube. I have already said in Part One that I am not happy about keeping catfish in the conventional way. I have shown the stringer method to a number of anglers who were against the idea at first, and all now use it having seen how effective it is and having been able to see that the fish is not damaged by its use.

You need a length of thin nylon rope, at least 7 metres long, which is about 22 feet. If you use anything shorter you could damage the fish as it needs to be able to rest on the bottom. Put one end of the rope through the mouth, and out of one of the gill covers. Make a loop and tie the type of knot which will not slip back onto the fish's mouth. The part round the fish should be quite loose, so that the teeth won't wear through it, and so that the rope will not be pulled tightly round the jaw of the fish. At first we used to make a small hole through the lower jaw of the fish to put the rope through, but we have now found that the tope tied as described will not damage the mouth or gill rakers of the fish.

What actually happens is that as long as they have plenty of rope, the fish on the stringer will go down to the bottom and lie still, realising

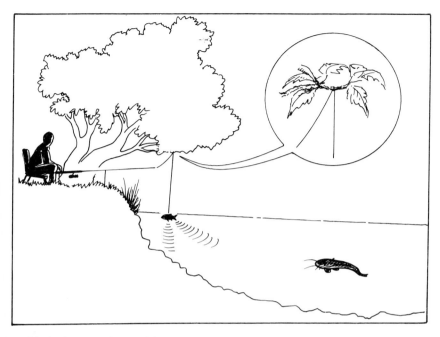

Livebating on surface at night
This is a very effective method used on the Continent on warm nights when catfish
are feeding near the surface.

from the pull on its mouth that it cannot escape. In this way, they get
a good rest from the hard fight,and can be very carefully pulled in when
the fish is to be returned. Needless to say, I would not use this, or any
other method of retention unless it was essential for me to keep the fish
for later weighing and photographing, and many of my catfish are returned
to the water at once, as I have said before. However, if I do occasionally
need to keep a big fish for accurate weighing or photographs, I will use
the stringer method—I once found one of my catfish nearly dead in a
big tube and had to support it in the water for three hours before if
recovered and swam away, but every fish I have put on a stringer has
gone back and swam sway happily without any damage at all. Fish such
as the 54 pounder mentioned above, do not get enough water exchange
in the tube to recover after all the effort they use in the fight, but with
a stringer they can recover in the water without being enveloped in a
sack which limits the amount of oxygen they can extract from the water.
A large, exhausted fish requires a lot of oxygen to recover and being

retained on a stringer allows them the maximum possible.

If you are still not happy about using this method, get someone who is used to it to show you exactly how it is done—or don't keep the fish at all, for any reason. And remember. . .give them plenty of rope, at least five metres in the water, and they will come to no harm if kept for a few hours.

France

In France *Silurus glanis* is known as the silure—a lovely name and one which I think we should adopt in England. To call Silurus glanis a 'catfish', as we do in the UK., is rather silly as there are more than 2000 species of catfish in the world. Silure, or silurus, would be a smashing name to use in England but we English are loath to change so do doubt 'catfish' it will stay.

The French might have the name right but that's where it stops. Most ordinary French anglers don't want the silure more widespread and they kill any that they catch. In towns along the banks of the River

There's no doubt what this silure has been eating; most French catfish are found to be passing out crushed up crayfish.

Saone, their best catfish venue, you will see lines of anglers and a lot of these fish for zander. They mistakenly believe the silure are gobbing up all the zander and because the anglers themselves want to kill every zander, the silure most die also! How wrong they are, but it would be impossible for us to try and educate them. The true facts are that the main diet of the Saone catfish is crayfish; nearly every time you catch one it is emitting crushed up crayfish. They also take the occasional roach and carp but I suspect they rarely take zander. With the lazy silure feeding on crayfish and anything else that it can scavenge, such as swan mussels that also abound in the river, it is probably *helping* their zander fishing!

The silure is a relatively 'new' fish to France and has only become really established in the last 20 years. French anglers, including the specimen hunters amongst them, are not inclined to move fish and so the silure is only found in quantity in two areas; the Loire valley and the Saone and its tributaries. Apart from this only a handful of other fisheries hold silure and these include a lake at Metz in northern France, one or two lakes in the Loire valley and some lakes near the Saone. Odd specimens have popped up in other places, such as from the mighty River Seine, but at present these can be ignored.

The River Loire is some 400 miles long and runs from the Lyon area northwards through Roanne and Nevers and then west through Orleans (60 miles south of Paris), Tours, Angers and out to sea at Nantes. I have not yet fished the Loire but from records I have collected the best areas are in the 150 mile stretch from Decize to Blois with Decize, Fourchambault, St. Laurent des Eaux and Gien regularly producing silure in the 50 pound plus class. English anglers would do well to visit this river as it is not such a long drive as some of the other venues in France and Spain and the Loire has produced several cats over 100 pounds. It is worth remembering that very few anglers in France wish to catch silure and there must be scores of places where some fantastic fishing is to be had—if you've got the chance to go, go now before it's too late!

The other main venue in France is the River Saone. The story goes that somewhere on the upper reaches of the River Sielle a Frenchman stocked some small silure into a private water about 30 years ago. Eventually they escaped into the warm, murky waters of the Sielle where they grew rapidly and bred prolifically. It wasn't long before the cats reached 100 pounds in this relatively small river and with the Sielle running into the Saone at Tournus the inevitable happened. Once into the might Saone the future of silure was safe and from here they spread downstream to Lyon and upstream past Chalon—a stretch of some 100 miles. Their spread has slowed down in recent years due to pollution from where the Rhone joins the Saone at Lyon and northwards of Chalon were the river decreases in size as it nears its source. However, 100 miles of excellent catfishing is plenty enough for any amount of English anglers that want to go.

It was in 1987 that I first visited France for catfish and although the following story has already been published I think it serves a good purpose to reprint it here. This then covers the River Sielle and a further story of my first session on the River Saone will give the reader a good insight as to the quality of fishing that is available.

'Mr. Nice Guy' was responsible for my first taste of continental catfishing. Anyone who has met Paul Regent from Seasalter in Kent will know why I've given him this name! Paul and I had already discovered Lake Cassien for English anglers and we have also been to Czechoslovakia on two occasions in search of 'sumec' (the Czech name for *Silurus glanis*). It therefore wasn't surprising that as soon as he had some information on silure, we were on our way together with our good friend Paul Nash.

One of Paul's contacts, Jackie Greset, a top match angler and tackle shop proprietor in Chalon, had advised us where to start. We did exactly what we were told and after a seven hour drive from Calais we found ourselves standing at a spot on the River Sielle about 40 yards wide with some fallen trees on the opposite bank. There was a slight flow and the water was a light brown colour, about the colour of Claydon Lakes! I quickly attached a lead to a rod and line and after a few casts we discovered that the river was flat-bottomed, about 8–12 feet deep in most areas and completely clear of snags apart from the occasional fallen trees which were easily visible. My first impressions were that it was going to be an easy place to fish and I was surprised to hear that quite a lot of big catfish were lost by French anglers. Apparently, several had been hooked close to fallen trees but the fish had 'waddled off' into these snags and even with heavy tackle they often couldn't be stopped.

As we'd taken to bait our first job was to catch a few fish to that live and dead baits could be used. This proved a little difficult at first, mainly due to us being useless 'float bashers'. Whilst the two Pauls tried various places I did my best to avoid float fishing and started to do a little scooping with a large landing net. The first scoop produced a few small fish and to my delight Paul said that there was a small catfish in the bottom of the mesh. He excitedly handed it to me whereupon I was horrified at what I could see. My heart sank to my boots and immediately I asked Paul if he's made sure that the reported captures were wels and not another species of catfish, for this little think was not a *Silurus glanis*! Paul's answer was, 'No, I didn't, but it doesn't matter does it as long as they're big?' I didn't know what to say next—for some reason I felt uninterested, despite their size, if they were not wels. Several further scoops produced more of these 'aliens', which were channel catfish, and a strong doubt set in my mind. I had not emphasised to Paul to check on the exact species—I automatically assumed by their sheer size that they must be wels. The more I thought about it the better I felt because there were cats to over 100 pounds in the river and I didn't know of another species of catfish in Europe that reached that size.

By the time we had caught a few fish, albeit quite small, there was only about three hours of daylight remaining and we had no action. We slept in and around the car that night and returned to our swims at dawn to next day. Most rods were cast alongside fallen trees with legered deadbait or paternostered live baits. Crayfish, which were easily scooped by landing net, were also used. The second day also produced no action and so we were looking forward to the third day when a couple of Paul's contacts were coming to see us.

Paul's friends arrived and it was pleasing to know that they were a little surprised that we had not hooked a catfish—it was obvious from this that we could expect some action during the week. Most of the day was spent chatting and sampling 'top' French wines and we looked at other parts of the river, the majority of which looked the same with only the occasional bend, a fallen true or a slightly deeper area adding a little interest. There were few holding areas and it was obvious from the amount of catfish caught that they must be spread throughout the river in open water. Our friends told us of one angler who had landed 70 silure the previous season averaging 60 pounds and we were absolutely amazed at this even if it was an exaggeration. Apparently he was a retired gentleman who specialised in catfish especially in the spring and early autumn—he considered mid-summer to be not worthwhile. It was now July!

We settled into our new swims for the remaining four hours, which were about 400 yards upstream or our first choice, and I felt very confident—if one angler can catch 70 in a year without fishing the hottest months we should at least be able to hook one, I thought! Our friends confirmed that although virtually no-one fished for the catfish in high summer, because of the extreme heat, we should get a couple of chances. This new area looked good, Paul fished the most likely looking area to the left with his baits only inches from some large fallen trees, Paul Nash to my right in a similar situation but I was lumbered with open water fishing. This didn't worry me very much because this was a reccé trip with the sole object of discovering whether it was worth Paul organising coach trips to the area and it didn't matter who got the action as long as we got some!

We again slept in and around the car that night and our 'new' baits were re-cast at dawn. We had been given some carp between half and one pound in weight and these were retained in a keepnet. About two hours after dawn, around 8am, Paul Regent shouted out and we'd hooked our first 'monster'. The fish had taken a live carp positioned close to a huge tree. Paul laid into the fish to get it away from the snags, his rod took up its full fighting curve but shortly after the hook pulled out. We were of course very disappointed—we inspected the tackle and everything looked right and we realised that the catfish must have had the fish only in its lips when Paul struck. There was nothing we could do about it however, because he would have to strike immediately otherwise the catfish would soon be back under the trees. We considered that a two hook rig might have caught that fish but we were concerned that we intended to return the catfish unharmed and were worried that previously uncaught fish might immediately swallow the bait and hooks. We decided to continue using a large single hook until we learnt more. It was at this stage that I decided to change my three rods over to Bob Baldock's polyball rig. We had been using a paternoster set-up on the advice of the French anglers but this kept tangling when used with a heavy braided hooklink and I could see no advantages of using the set-up. My rig was now a large single hook about 2/0 in size, with a three quarter inch polystyrene ball tied to it, two 24 inch lengths of Millward's 'medium' fly line backing (which at that time I used in England) side by side, a large swivel and bead to stop a three ounce running lead which was attached via a 2 inch nylon link. Between main swivel and lead link was a 3 inch length of plastic tubing to stop the lead link tangling with the twin braided hook link. I decided to use two strands of hook length because there was a chance that we'd be playing a large catfish for quite a time and the hooklink could be subjected to considerable wear when continually moving across the mouth against the rows of needle-like teeth. I had tested this at home and two lengths easily outlasted a single heavier length. (Nowadays, when I go abroad, I always use a heavy monofilament hooklink around 40 pounds B.S. The big cats in most European countries are not returned after capture and therefore are not line shy). Main line was 20 pound B. S. Polyarn from Simpsons of Turnford and I must say that this is an excellent line for the job—soft, very abrasive-resistant and very cheap. The rest of the day remained uneventful but we found the incredible variety of large home-made boats that cruised past most amusing. Some looked as if they could sink at any moment and there were some weird and wonderful designs with caravans and tents on top! Some boasted topless girls and loud disco music blaring out. I just kept saying to myself, 'If the French can catch them in these circumstances so can we!'

The start of the following day was a carbon copy of the previous— about two hours after dawn we had another take, but this time to one of my rods cast in open water. I had previously 'checked' the movements of the livebait by adjusting the baitrunning mechanism of the Shimano 4500 so that the live bait couldn't quite take line off the reel. With no indicators, apart from Optonics, a large catfish would feel virtually no resistance on taking the bait, and set up in this way no false 'bites' would

River Sielle – small river, big cats and big boats!

occur. The first thing I heard was a short but fast take of about two feet to my middle rod as a catfish seized the bait. After two or three seconds of no movement the line went out slow and steadily. I was sitting right by my rods and struck immediately when the run started. I knew exactly what had happened, for most of the catfish I've caught on the polyball rig in England have done the same thing. My strike, although hard and fast, only resulted in the rod being half bent as the fish was probably moving towards me so I wound down and pulled into the cat very hard putting a full bend into the rod. Once I was happy that the hook was set I eased off knowing full well what happens if you give a catfish a lot of stick! Paul Nash quickly wound all the rods in whilst the other Paul started the video camera. The fish moved off slowly to the left going down river and taking line from the clutch. I had no intention of stopping it as there was plenty of open water about. The cat had only taken about 15 yards of line when it decided to turn around and proceed in an opposite direction whereupon it went for about 30 yards through Paul Nash's swim towards a fallen tree. A slight increase in pressure persuaded it to turn again an it was soon in front of me. As we got the fish nearer there was a huge swirl on top and about three

Peter Ploetz assists Kevin with his 54-pounder from the Schnackensee fishery in Germany.

One of Schnackensee's feeding sprees produced these 'small' waller of $34\frac{1}{2}$ pounds for Brenda Maddocks, a 25-pound albino for Peter Wilson and a $36\frac{1}{2}$ for Kevin.

The River Rott, in the beautiful Bavarian countryside, yielded these two waller of 29 pounds to Kevin and 35 pounds to Bill Turner. Both fish took a bunch of lobworms.

A dream come true – 113 pounds of hard-fighting, tail-waving waller from Schnackensee in July 1990. With two-, three- and four-man-cats the captor always holds the head end. The German angler in the middle had landed a 150-pounder two hours earlier!

Paul Nash and Paul Regent help support Kevin's three-man silure of 79 pounds from the River Sielle in France.

Bob Baldock with his hard-earned 70-pounder from the River Saone in France.

Three leeches suspended 18 inches off the bottom tempted this River Saone 39 after all other baits failed.

Bob assists Kevin with his 74-pound siluro from the Ebro that took nearly two hours to subdue.

The result of three angler's efforts on the River Sielle for a whole week – one silure of exactly 30 pounds.

Keith Lambert displays his personal best – a 61-pound silure from the River Saone between Tournus and Macon.

Robert Coote flexes his muscles with this fabulous 65-pounder from the Ebro which was a short-lived personal best; Robert landed a 69 a few days later!

Kevin carefully returns a lucky 69-pounder to the Ebro to fight another day. Had it picked up a Spaniard's bait, it probably would have been killed.

One of the many fish caught whilst making the video CAT FEVER; this one went 45 pounds and took a small carp.

The end of an incredible week's filming in France and Spain – Kevin and Bob with siluro of $97\frac{1}{2}$ and 67 pounds. The biggest fish was $1\frac{1}{2}$ pounds short of the Spanish record and both are featured in CAT FEVER: THE VIDEO.

Kevin with the first big siluro taken on 'revised' boat tackle. This 82-pounder took only
15 minutes to subdue on a powerful 9-foot boat rod.

feet of tail waved in the air. 'How big is it?' the two Pauls asked—I
had only seen its rear half and none of the 'business end' so I had to
take a guess at its minimum weight. 'At least 40 pounds', I said. Paul
Nash was none too pleased about this for he was by now holding my
huge landing net which has five-foot arms. I knew Paul was a little appre-
hensive about handling a huge fish so I threw in another statement for
good measure: 'You'll have a job to get it in there Paul!'. He worriedly
muttered something but I didn't catch what he said for as the fish rolled
it pulled away a little faster against the clutch, bending double the two
and three quarter pound test curve compound carbon. Not wanting to
upset the fish I let it do what it wanted and it was soon in front of
us again. Until now I had not put any real pressure on the fish—I had
'kidded' it in, like you can often do with a big English cat, and I was
hoping that this fish wouldn't realise it before we got it in the net. All
of a sudden a huge head broke surface about 10 feet in front of the
landing net and whilst I stood there open-mouthed at the colossal size
of the thing Paul dropped the net and walked backwards a little! 'Don't
worry about its size', I said, 'just keep the net still and don't move it
until I've pulled its head against the spreader block'. Paul Regent was
still operating the video camera and after swearing about its size, which
didn't help matters, he said he couldn't fit it all in the lens! Once the
beast was on top I slowly walked backwards pulling it over the waiting
net, just 20 minutes after hooking, and as soon as its head touched the
net's block Paul started to lift the net. I immediately threw the rod onto
the ground and rushed to Paul's assistance knowing that we had to lift
the net carefully otherwise it could easily slide back over the front cord.
We scooped it into the net and dragged it ashore well up the bank. 'Must
be 80–90 pounds', I said.

For a few moments we all stood there in amazement, our eyes fixed
on this huge, placid-looking silure as it lay there motionless. The large
single hook was embedded about 3 inches inside the mouth and was
easily removed. We were not sure how to weigh it properly—it was far
too big for the weighing sling so we removed the pole from the landing
net and after a few minor problems settled for a weight of 79 pounds—a
little over average size for the river!

We didn't have a proper tape measure so Paul Nash laid a rod alongside the fish, marked it and measured it later and the catfish, which was
a female, turned out to be exactly six feet in length. A few photographs
were taken and it then was decided to sack the fish until our French
friends arrived later. However, the catfish was not happy in the 'small'
sack and it lay on its side all the time and it would obviously perish
if left as it was. We decided that we must try to retain the fish as we'd
promised to show any to our friends that had helped us so much. They
had kept all their promises and we felt we couldn't let them down but

we were also determined to return the fish alive. The main problem was the size of the sack, so Paul Regent cut the bottom out of a spare sack and then sewed two together making a huge one. We transferred the silure to the new sack and although at first the fish would not right itself, after 30 minutes of holding it upright it eventually settled down quite happily. Another photographic session followed later in the day and it gave me great pleasure to be the first angler ever to return a catfish live to the river. As the fish swam away I thought to myself that I bet it would fight a lot harder the next time it was hooked!

We fished another two days and apart from a definite catfish run to a dead bream which I failed to contact with on the strike, we had no more action. In about five days fishing we'd had three definite catfish takes with another two possibles—not bad I thought for one of the worst times of the year and with no knowledge of the water.

However, it transpired after another three of four visits of catching only two more decent fish, that we had discovered this water too late; the local French anglers had caught and killed many of the catfish. I never met a French angler who returned the fish. Once told me he fed them to his cats and dogs. Another told me that he always cut out the gill rakers, so that they bled to death, and he then three them back in the river!

Fortunately, before being heavily persecuted the silure had got into the Saone and were by now well established. On one trip we were told of a lake in Macon, called Le Darce, which is attached to the Saone where some huge catches of catfish had been made. We spent two short days there and saw lots of big carp but we didn't have the time to fish it properly but it looks a likely venue, especially the entrance area of several acres that we did not fish. I have always wanted to return to that place and another a little downstream where there is a long island and a slack, but life is too short to be able to fish everywhere!

Unbeknown to me, the opportunity to return to the Saone occurred suddenly in August 1990. As already mentioned, I had always hoped to be able to find time to fish the Saone but never expected to actually get there—other venues in Germany, Spain, Russia and Romania were calling!

Just 12 hours before a party of eight of us were due to embark on a ten day catfishing expedition to the Danube Delta in Romania, it was called off. Apparently there had been an outbreak of cholera in the Delta area and we were not welcome. So strong was our desire to catch huge cats that we still insisted on going and arranged for 'last minute' injections but the Delta men refused to have us!

What was good news for the wives and girlfriends was short lived. An emergency meeting was called for and I persuaded the rest of the lads, most of whom were highly experienced catfish anglers, that we should try the Saone.

The following evening found five of us on the banks of the Saone between Tournus and Macon—the other three, Paul Nash, Bill Turner and Mick Barnard had opted to fish for carp at a lake nearby. We were delighted to find that the river was not in flood and our contingency plans of continuing to Spain weren't called for. Crazy isn't it? 12 hours earlier we didn't know if we were going to Romania, France of Spain!

We spent four or five hours in heatwave conditions looking at as many spots of the river as possible by which time we virtually 'collapsed' into the spot we fancied.

Bob Baldock, Robert Coote, Keith Lambert, Simon Clarke and myself spread out along a 150 yard stretch of river using three rods each. Baits for the first evening and morning sessions were perfect carp and tench laid on by Keith, which we'd brought with us pumped up in oxygen bags. Rigs were link leger in the main, with and without polyball, whilst Bob tried a paternoster. The river was about 300 yards wide at that spot and baits were cast at varying distances between 10—40 yards. I was fishing alongside Simon (because he keeps me amused!).

We didn't have to wait long for our first bite; about an hour after dark Simon had a good steady run on tench and struck into a cat. Unfortunately, after about half a minute's battle it came unhooked. It was simply a case that Simon had almost certainly hooked it in the teeth and when this happens the hook doesn't penetrate and then falls out sometime during the fight. Although it was upsetting, it was also exciting news to hook one so soon after starting in a spot we'd never fished before.

The following day was spent finding out as much as possible about the river. It was about 25 feet deep in the centre with gradual slopes going down to this boat channel which had a flat bottom for about 20 yards. The margins were a little rocky with the occasional small weedbeds close in. The river bed was covered in crayfish and mussels and the water was like the Sielle—a dirty brown colour with all sorts of things floating past! They looked like worm's sleeping bags to me but Simon informed me in a posh voice that they were 'condoms'. At this stage the others stopped using the river water for tea making etc, but I carried on as usual!

We had no action through the day but shortly after dark Keith hooked into our first biggy on a tench livebait and it went 61 pounds. A personal best for Keith and we were all excited at the prospects. At dawn the next morning Simon had his second run but not having a Bait-trunner reel cost him what was certainly his biggest ever cat. Simon was fishing straight off the clutch which meant that he would need to tighten it up before playing the fish properly. On the strike he trapped the line against the rod and struck into the fish perfectly. The cat immediately moved away quickly and with that incredible power that they have. After striking, Simon had to release the line and then adjust his clutch but between this happening there was about one second with less pressure on the fish at which time the spool over-ran and caused a bird's nest. The fish pulled Simon into the water up to his waist, his rod was pulled lower and lower until it pointed at the fish, followed by a loud crack as the new 26lb line parted on a straight pull! As I've always said, there is nothing that can stop a big cat on its first run (if it decides to go) and you have to be prepared for this to happen at any minute when fishing on the Continent.

The weather continued hot and again nothing happened throughout the day for us except for runs caused by the huge barges that frequent the river. They pass backwards and forwards all day and when they're fully loaded down to within six inches of the water level the displacement of water is unbelievable; a drop and rise in the river water of up to three feet occurs as some of these boats pass. At this stage everybody gets runs and the keepnets are washed ashore! We did witness a silure of about 45 pounds which a Frenchman caught from a boat after only two hours fishing at mid-morning. He caught it on paternostered roach and we walked along the bank to have a look at it. We didn't stay long as the angler had gaffed it horribly and was about to despatch it!

We decided to continue in the same swims but Robert and I agreed that we'd move to the opposite bank the next day. Nothing happened after dark which surprised me but early morning Keith had another fish, this time a 24½ pounder, again on tench. Four hours later I had my first run and hooked into a good silure. It ran out to the middle of the river and fought doggedly making another two or three short runs during the fight which lasted about 15 minutes. My first Saone cat was in the net and a nice one too at 45 pounds. The fish had taken a poly-balled tench.

Robert and I moved to the opposite side, which was little fished, at mid-day and set up on a rocky island which had appeared due to low water. It consisted of huge rocks and was only just big enough to take our gear. It came to light later that we completely forgot to consider the rise and fall in the water level that the barges create!

In the next two days Robert and I had a lot of action on our 'wet and dry' island and we landed several cats but unfortunately the biggest only went about 15 pounds. Robert actually had one take his bait as he was retrieving it but that one came off.

We were now approaching the end of our stay and with two days left Bob still hadn't had a run and Simon was still fishless. A move was called for and the rest of the gang moved to our side of the river. It was a very awkward bank and so overgrown that it was impossible to cast from the swims but with 'water baby' Simon around this created no problem. Simon, who's often in the water, waded out and cast Keith's,

Kevin's first River Saone silure of 45 pounds which took a suspended tench.

Bob's and his ownbaits out towards the centre channel.

This move was to change their luck and within two hours Bob connected with his first Saone silure which had taken a small carp. After a very powerful and exciting fight Bob landed his personal best, a magnificent looking fish of 70 pounds. A little later Simon had a 19 and everybody was happy.

Robert and I continued catching small ones and Keith lost two on some rocks in front of him. On the last day we saw another French angler boat fishing and he caught a 45 and a 90! All in all it was a very successful trip especially as we'd never fished the Saone before. We fished an area close to town where the silure had quite obviously been persecuted over the years. This means that there *must* be some excellent areas along the Saone, much better than where we'd fished. Out of town there are some lovely looking spots where no-one fishes and these areas must be teeming with catfish.

In September 1990 Bob and I re-visited the same spot for a short session on our way to Spain whilst making the video film *Cat Fever* and I managed to get a 39 pounder. So there you have it; 100 miles of excellent river holding silure to at least 150 pounds—what more could you ask for so close to home?

Germany

In northern Germany *Silurus glanis* is known as the 'wels' but in the beautiful Bavarian countryside this fantastic fish is referred to as the 'waller'.

Waller are very common in southern Germany but not so in the north where there are many areas that contain none. Unlike France and Spain, it would be impossible to list most of the catfish waters for two reasons; firstly, there are hundreds and secondly, I don't know them all!

The three main rivers which consistently produce big catfish are the Regen, Naab and Donau (Danube to us) which are all south east of Nurnberg. I have spent some time looking at various spots on these rivers and I would love to fish them all but as I often say, life is too short to be able to fish everywhere. The waller in the Naab suffered from a mystery pollution some years ago when most of the fish perished and although they have made a recovery it would be better to concentrate on the Regen or Danube. The record for the Naab is a 143 pounder caught in 1983. The River Regen has produced fish well in excess of 100 pounds but the best spots are often kept secret by local anglers. These areas are undoubtedly between Cham and Regensburg and along this stretch there are several dams. For a considerable distance below the dams the water tends to be very shallow but above these it is the deeper, slower stretches that the waller prefer. If I were to fish this relatively small river, I would do it by boat as much of the banks are privately owned. I would echo-sound it and spend say 24 hours, fishing each deep area and I don't think it would take long to locate the better fish.

The mighty River Danube is of course a completely different prospect to the Naab and Regen and I should think the big waller are not so concentrated and can be caught virtually anywhere. As with the Regen, it would be better to fish this river by boat as the banks are inaccessible in many places. Hoteliers and restaurant owners charge a lot for fishing and usually don't allow night fishing. One must also remember that, like the Saone in France, it is a busy river with lots of boats and people about. The Regen is quite the opposite with lots of quiet places and very few boats.

This 103 pounder was caught from the Thenner Lake, near Munich in 1983 and measured 6½ feet.

As already mentioned there are catfish in hundreds of waters in Germany. Another good friend of mine, Jurgen Paul, who lives in Frankfurt, lives close to an excellent venue, the River Main. There are many waller in this large river and at one spot where a warm water outlet of a power station joins the river it is possible to catch large specimens in the middle of winter.

In 1989 I accepted an invitation from Jurgen to join him for a few days catfishing on the River Rott. This small river runs close to the German/Austrian border before joining the Danube at Passau. The stretch of river we were to fish was owned by a hotel and the fishing was free as long as you stayed at the hotel. Our party was made up of my wife, daughter and I plus Robert Coote and Bill Turner. We had only known Bill a few weeks but the combination of him being a jolly nice chap and having just been given a week off work made him an obvious contender!

We met Jurgen and his friend, Ben, at the hotel and two rooms were soon booked. With Brenda and Jacqueline sleeping in the hotel as well as Jurgen doing the same, due to his physical disability, it would keep the owners happy enough, especially if we others came back for the occasional slap up meal.

After booking the rooms I went back to the car for our suitcases and I noticed a garage door had swung open and I could see a large fish tank. I walked over and was surprised to find some large bream and several catfish to 10 pounds in the tank. Quite naively I was concerned at how overcrowded the tank was and surprised that any of them were alive in such appalling conditions. I was then joined by the head chef who told me in broken English that they were to be cooked tonight for the guests!

Before getting over that shock, one of the hotel staff was instructed to take us along the river in the hotel's boat because we were not sure where to start fishing. Five of us got into a punt and as we were smartly pushed off out into the river a long line of water fountains appeared inside the boat through a gap in the planks. Not knowing any German, I pointed at these water jets, open mouthed and was promptly handed a bailing bucket! The next 20 minutes was spent bailing out water as quickly as possible until I lost the battle and the boat sank! I couldn't believe it, here we were, standing in the river, soaking wet, with no fishing tackle and back at the hotel was catfish waiting to be cooked for supper—something wrong here I thought!

We fished an area for two days but had no action so we borrowed a different boat and spent some time looking at the rest of the hotel's stretch. At last we found what we were looking for and we settled into that spot for the remaining three days of our trip. We had found three metres of water close to a bank where the river turned sharply. This

A partly digested rat coughed up by a mere 6 pound catfish.

bank had obviously suffered some erosion over the years and had been reinforced with large rocks. Adjacent to this deep water, on the inside of the bend, was some very shallow water. Downstream of the bend was a straight stretch of unfishable river about two metres deep and 300 metres long. Perfect we thought—a nice deep area where the cats can lie up with some shallows close by where the cats might choose to feed. All five of us spread ourselves out around the bend and I chose to fish an awkward spot at the start of the long piece of unfished water. Baits were live roach and bream, crayfish, lobworms and maulwarfsgrille. Initially, we persisted with livebaits to no avail until the second day when I caught our first Rott catfish of about six pounds on a big bunch of lobworms. I popped the fish into a tube for a few minutes whilst we organised our cameras and was surprised to find a coughed-up rat in the bottom of the tube!

We started to use lobworms more and a little after dark the next day Bill had a run, and boy did we hear about it? I should explain that Bill had never caught a catfish before and this 'thing' nearly pulled him in. What I would have given for a tape recorder that night—Bill was in a different world and the explanations were pouring from his mouth as he back-wound his reel as quick as possible in the pitch darkness. The waller had moved out into the current and was heading down stream and there was nothing Bill could do to stop it. Eventually it slowed down and a more dogged fight continued. At regular intervals throughout the battle Bill kept saying he'd never felt anything like this and some 30 minutes after hooking I slipped the net under his first catfish. Robert and I struggled with it up the awkward bank and Bill nearly wet himself when the torches suddenly illuminated his catch. These moments are rare in fishing and we were as pleased as Bill was. The fish weighed 35 pounds and we decided to retain it for pictures the next morning. It had taken lobworms again, so all remaining rods were changed over to large bunches of worms—as many as we could get on a 5/0 hook.

A few hours later Robert caught one about 8 pounds but it wasn't until a couple of hours after light that we connected with our next decent waller. I had a violent take on a worm bait placed only one rod length from my bank and after a very exciting fight we banked a lovely looking 29 pounder. As Brenda was still at the hotel we decided to keep the fish until she arrived but when Brenda returned we had a terrible problem. She had quite innocently mentioned to the hotel staff that Bill had caught a 35 pounder and they ordered us to bring the fish back to the hotel for cooking. Apparently this was normal practice—the fish belonged to the hotel and anything caught was to be put on the menu. Being typically English, there was no way Bill's fish was ending up in the oven but we didn't want to spoil Jurgen's relationship with the hotel. Eventually, we were told that the waller was worth £150 to the hotel and we bargained with them until they accepted £90 from us so that we could return the fish! At this rate we couldn't afford to catch any more and we were praying that they didn't know about the 29 pounder. When everything was settled we sped off down river with the cats in the boot of the car to photograph them together.

Our welcome came to an end later that day after I was severely reprimanded for returning several big bream that had taken my lobworms. The owner was already annoyed about losing out on Bill's fish and so desperately wanted to cook the bream that he made it obvious we were not welcome. We settled out bills and promptly left thereby ending our happy experiences on the River Rott.

Another place in Germany that I've fished for waller is the famous Schnackensee fishery at Gunzenhausen, about 25 miles south of Nurnberg.

Schnackensee is a day-ticket water, and is primarily a 'put and take' carp fishery, run in somewhat the same way as we run trout fisheries of this kind in England. It is stocked with carp on a fairly regular basis, especially in the autumn, and most of the carp caught are taken away and eaten. The owner, Werner Vogel, is interested in catfish, and has stocked Schnackensee with some very large fish from Eastern Europe. He tries to ensure that the big ones are not killed—you can take small ones, but if your catfish is over 20lb it will cost you a lot of money per pound to kill it and take it away.

There are carp to 33lb and catfish to 150lb in the lake, and also grass carp to 30lb, pike to about the same weight, zander to 16lb and roach, bream etc.

The lake is about eight acres in size, and there is no night fishing. You can only fish from one hour before sunrise to one hour after sunset. The other disadvantage is that as it is a day-ticket water, it is packed at week-ends, although nothing like as crowded during the week. Day tickets cost about £8 for two rods, and there is an area for tents and bivvies at £3 per day, and about £6 per day for caravans. There is also a small guest house beside the lake where you can get bed and breakfast for about £10 a night, and there is a hotel nearby at about the same price.

One of the things which impressed me the most about the place was the large size of the catfish compared with the small size of the lake, and plenty of those fish are over 100lbs in weight. This is an excellent place for the English to go and catch a very big catfish. You can leave home, and the same day be setting up your rods with these big catfish swimming around your bait.

Go into the bar of the guest house as soon as you get there and have a look at the many impressive photographs round the walls. They show some huge catfish ... and you'll want to get fishing. There's plenty of good food here, with the average meal costing about £5, and even the beer is good.

It's a very easy carp water and you'll get several fish a day, mostly between 4 and 10lbs, with some doubles and the odd 20, but I go for the catfish. Fish baits, bunches of worms, maulwarfsgrille and mussels are the commonest baits used, though fish baits are very good, and so is the type of leech used by the Germans, the blutegal. In hot weather the fish seem to feed all day and the best months are usually June, July and August, with July the best of all.

On my first day in July 1989, I was met by an extraordinary sight. In the middle of the lake I could see huge catfish tails, moving slowly as the big fish felt with their feelers along the bottom in the shallow water. What a sight—I couldn't believe it at first. They were feeding too, in the 4½ feet deep water—catfish of 6ft long with their tails out of the water. It's a good 150 yards to the middle—too far to cast—but towards the evening the catfish came into the margins. Although they couldn't actually be seen in the opaque water, big swirls were visible as the catfish chased the carp. This really gets you going; you're sure you will get a take at any minute. Just imagine the water displacement caused by a hundred pound fish, and you'll get the picture—heart pounding stuff!

As there are no snags, ordinary carp rods with line of from 15–18lbs BS can be used, and with monofilament straight to the hook. Like most

The notice board at Schnackensee.

continental catfish waters, no special types of rigs or hook links are needed. I use a Sylcast hook length of 26 lbs breaking strain, in case of a long fight, in which the line could get frayed across the small teeth of the big cats. Beware of using very flexible hook links as livebaits can tie incredible knots in them. My first catfish was caught on three or four large leeches on a 8/0 hook, 'popped-up' off the bottom with a polyball, legered well out. A German angler showed me how he got a tench livebait to swim well out into the lake, fishing it freeline, and 'teasing' it into swimming further out by pulling on the line to make it swim in the opposite direction, when it would go at least 100 yards. This method was very successful when the catfish were in the middle.

As the Green Party is very strong in Germany, they have managed to get a law passed which says that all fish must be killed. It is considered to be tormenting the fish to catch and to return them. Needless to say, many German anglers don't agree with this law, and I don't agree with it either, preferring to return fish than to beat their heads in. That law also means that it is illegal in Germany to use livebaits. Many German anglers still do use them, but they do it discreetly.

That first catfish was only about 7 lb but I then had a couple of doubles, and finally I was fortunate enough to get a 54 pounder, though even this was not a big fish for Schnackensee. Just before dark proved to be a very good time, and most of the fish were caught at this time. It got quite cold whilst I was there, and there was little feeding during the daytime. I finished up with 12 catfish over the five days, and my German friend Peter Ploetz had about the same number.

I found the fishing very enjoyable, and the owners and anglers who fished there are very friendly. There is a very small tackle shop nearby where you can buy some items, and even a few boilies are sold (Maestros, of course) and you can also buy rod licences here. Angling standards are not very good, with many local anglers using crude methods, so a good angler using English methods tends to catch plenty of fish.

Schnackensee fishing can only be regarded as fairly light-hearted, not too serious fishing, because it is quite acrowded water, but this is not very important if you want a big catfish. My 'small' 54 pounder was quite a bit bigger than the British record ... and who cares about a bit of overcrowding when there's a good chance of catching a fish over 100 lbs?

If you do go to Schnackensee to fish, you will need to accept the fact that you are in a different country, with different ideas. You will see double figure carp caught, killed, taken over to the barbecue area, cleaned, cooked and eaten on the spot—common practice in many countries, including France and Spain, as well as in Germany. Since the fish are plentiful and are used for food, I can see no objection to this, but I do get upset when I see big fish killed and just thrown into the bushes, which also happens sometimes in other countries, and did here, for that matter, until the late forties.

The fish are often treated badly too and you will have to get used to this in other countries. There is no difference between killing a carp or catfish for food, and an English sea angler killing a cod for the same reason. My advice is not to go there and try to tell the locals what to do.

However, this and the no night fishing rule are about the only disadvantages in Schnackensee fishing. It's a pleasant place, and as the fishing is not too serious you could take the family and have a good time, with perhaps some good catches as a reward. If you hook a very big fish, the owner or a bailiff will put a huge tub into your swim, and the fish is put into it, taken to the fishing hut where it is properly weighed, photographed and returned to the water.

What I find exciting about Schnackensee fishing is the freeline method; twitching the line between thumb and forefinger to feel the bait. At first I asked my German friend Peter how I would know I had a run, but I soon found out; squeeze the line in your fingers, and if it keeps going ... it's a waller. This is an unusual feeling for an English angler, as there the catfish don't drop the bait. The resistance simply doesn't seem to bother them. It was necessary to wait a minute or two before striking a fish, which I found very frustrating; if we struck earlier we sometimes missed fish, and even if they were left for several minutes it did no harm, as none had swallowed the baits.

You can just turn up and fish but if you want to book accommodation, you will need to write in advance—well in advance. You can sleep in your bivvie in the special area without booking, but all your gear must be taken off the lake at night. The address is: Schnackensee, Gunzenhausen, near Nurnberg, West Germany.

My second visit to Schnackensee was in July 1990. Brenda, Jacqueline and I were joined by one of the Withy Pool syndicate members, Peter Wilson and his fiancee Jayne. Peter and Jayne arrived on the Saturday, one day before us, the plan being to start fishing when the weekend crowds had gone. On arrival Peter informed us that there was a 24 hour match in progress the day before with more than 300 anglers taking part—all on an eight acre lake!

The plan was for Peter and I to fish for waller from Monday to Friday with Jayne mainly carp fishing and trying her hand for waller when she felt confident to do so, with Brenda having the odd go for both on occasions throughout the week. I should mention that Peter and Jayne are both highly experienced anglers, Peter having caught a 41 pound carp already that season with Jayne's best at 23¾ pounds. Peter had also caught several cats in England.

On the first day, Jayne immediately started to catch carp up to 14 pounds and I could see she was going to enjoy herself. Peter had the odd go for carp and eventually, late in the day, I cast out two lines for cats.

With odd sightseeing and shopping trips (we don't normally fish hard at Schnackensee) we didn't see any waller until the morning of the third day. Werner, the owner who always looks after us so well, suggested that we fish in one of the bays at the back of the lake and I then remembered that the waller moved into the same area the previous year when the banks were quiet. That morning Peter and I set up in the narrowest part of the lake and within a few minutes Peter had a take on tench. Shortly after hooking, the waller treated us to a tail waving session that shocked us all. I've seen many catfish tails waving but never a white one! The fish fought well and all the time Peter prayed that this rare catfish would stay on the hook. Everything went to plan and we soon had the ghost of a fish in the net. It was a truly impressive albino and weighed in at 25 pounds.

Our cameras were back at the rooms so Peter went back to fetch his and whilst he was gone I hooked our second waller on blutegals which turned out to be a 36½ pounder. Peter arrived in time to land the fish and we then decided that I'd best get my cameras. Whilst playing my cat, Brenda also hooked one which unfortunately broke her up, so Peter and Brenda continued while I went back to get the gear.

With the waller feeding so well I ran all the way and was shocked to find on my return that in the three or four minutes I'd been gone Brenda had hooked and landed another one, this time at 34½ pounds. We photographed the three fish together and shortly after this they went off the feed. Needless to say everyone was pleased, except for Jayne of course—she was out shopping! Jayne soon made up for it though by catching two cats over 20 the next morning in the same spot.

Towards the end of the week Brenda and Jayne decided that they wanted to 'slaughter' the carp for one day just to show off in front of the locals. We had taken a decent quantity of Maestro Boilies with us so Pete fired out three or four thousand of them. They were all spread out, but at the same distance over a wide area, so that all four carp rods could be case out at leisure in an arch. After that it was fireworks, the carp couldn't resist the Oceanic Oils and Strawberry Oil flavoured boilies and at one time I'm sure the water level was down with so many fish on the bank. Everybody around the lake stopped watching their own rods and couldn't take their eyes of the girls. Was it their legs, or was it the carp they kept looking at? It wasn't long before we were giving bags of boilies and Booster Dips away and more of the locals starting catching. It was great fun but the girls were unlucky size-wise with the biggest fish being only 19 pounds, caught by Brenda. One chap caught a 24 pounder on the bait—but that's fishing.

With only two days left which included a Saturday we still didn't have any big waller to our credit, although I'd managed one of 40 pounds and a mid-twenty, and Peter and Jayne had caught another small one each. Time was running out and the next day was spent long range fishing towards the middle with leeches where some cat's tails could be seen. Apart from a dropped take we finished the day biteless.

It was now Saturday—a day we'd intended not to fish because the lake is usually very busy at weekends. Brenda and I were leaving early the next morning and so we packed our gear away. Werner and his wife had kindly invited us all to a special catfish dinner and this was arranged for mid-afternoon. The meal was absolutely super and we sampled waller superbly cooked in three different ways. Just as we were finishing the meal, which we were having in Werner's garden very close to the lake, a message came back that an angler was playing a big waller which he'd hooked on leeches. Peter and I were excused and we watched the angler for about 20 minutes and although he had the right gear and knew what he was doing, he was making no impression on this big fish so we returned for some more wine. Messages kept coming back that the battle was still on, until finally about 1½ hours after hooking we were told it was landed. Werner always weighs the big fish properly on some special scales in a hut so we hurriedly went there. We looked at the fish which was in a big tub for carrying it round to the hut and I knew I was looking at the first cat I'd ever seen over 100 pounds. What impressed me most was not the length, which was about seven feet, but the incredible depth along the whole of its body—it was truly massive. The lake record had recently been beaten by a 12 year old boy and stood at about 135 pounds and we were shocked to find this fish weighed more. It was exactly 150 pounds, not only a new lake record but also the new unofficial German record!

I looked at the fish and then at the lake and I could see *and sense* that the really big ones were on the feed for the first time this week. I just had to fish even though there was only a couple of hours left. The ladies weren't keen, as our dinner had hardly gone down, but I told Peter that we'd got to and he agreed. As it happened this turned out to be one of the best decisions of my angling career. It's strange how things happen—the holiday was over, I'd packed my gear and the chances of catching a big one in a couple of hours after not getting one in a whole week, must have been slim.

Our baits were out for about 1½ hours when all of a sudden with only 30 minutes to go it happened. I had a good take on the long distance rod and I struck as hard as I could. Immediately the rod hopped over and as I stepped back there was a massive disturbance in the lake as half a huge catfish came out of the water. I was into one of the big ones . . .

Peter wound all the other rods in and for the next 30 minutes I played the fish very hard and had a most enjoyable fight. It was quite an active fish and went on several runs often displaying itself noisily as it changed direction. I was fishing off the side of one of the long spits and towards the end of the fight the leviathan decided to go round behind me into the back bay. This caused a few minutes excitement as Peter and I struggled to get the rod and line over several marginal bushes that were taller than us.

By now it was dark and the fight was being finished in the back bay. I told Peter he'd have to lift it out by hand as this one wouldn't fit into our net. He then reminded me that I'd promised to show him how to do it in the week but the opportunity hadn't arisen and now he was faced to do it in the dark with a fish bigger than himself! I carefully explained to Peter exactly how to do it and then repeated it three or four times. After about ten questions from Peter he seemed happy to give it a try—come to think of it he had no choice!

As the monster neared the bank its huge head appeared on the surface. Pete put his thumb into the waller's mouth but something went wrong, then Pete swore and the fish sped off out into the bay again completely soaking him in water. More confidence was called for and the next opportunity was not missed. As soon as Peter had hold of its mouth he shouted for help and we struggled up the bank with what was obviously a huge fish. We were both very excited and I looked after it as Peter ran round to get a tub and fetch Werner.

The fish was weighed accurately at 113 pounds and was 6 feet 7 inches long. We then photographed it and it was returned immediately. What a fish!

Spain

I suppose that many anglers might think that there have always been catfish in Spain but this is not so. Prior to 1974 there were no *Silurus glanis* in Spain which is quite amazing when you see how suitable their climate and rivers are for Europe's largest freshwater fish.

Followers of siluro have Roland Lorkowski to thank for their introduction to the River Ebro. A German biologist, tackle manufacturer and experienced angler, Roland carefully planned the stocking of the fish. Initially, some small fry were obtained from a fish farm and introduced into a lake in Köln. In 1974, nine of these small catfish were successfully moved to the Ebro and by mid '75 a total of 32 between 20–30cm (8–12″) had been introduced. The water had been carefully chosen and it would have been difficult to find a more suitable river anywhere else in Europe. The Ebro's warm waters flow at a leisurely pace as they cross the arid plains of Aragon. Extensive shallows, large areas of murky water and an absolute mass of small carp complete the recipe for the perfect catfish venue. From then on nature took its course and soon after the siluro were sexually mature, sometime in the early 80's, they successfully bred. For almost a decade, the secret of the siluro lurked at the bottom of the Ebro.

In 1984 a catfish of 15 pounds was caught accidentally on a dead rudd and the following year another of 30 pounds took a spoon intended for pike. All sorts of stories started to spread around the Ebro towns and the numerous bars were full of chat about the new 'monster' of the river. Of course the ones that got away weighed several hundred pounds and were longer than the bar-top!

One man who wasn't surprised at all was of course Roland, and in 1986 he and a friend set out to catch some specimens to see how they were progressing. Several siluro between 45 and 50 pounds were caught and by 1988 Roland had pushed the Spanish record up to more than 70 pounds. A growth rate of 10–15 pounds a year was evident; twice the normal rate for the species. As I write now, in October 1990, the record stands at 99 pounds.

The two most important factors that control the growth rate of *Silurus glanis* are water temperature and availability of food. This venue has very warm water for a good part of the year; growth is possible for nine months instead of the usual five or six months a year in Eastern Europe and perhaps only three months in England. In Spain they have been caught accidentally by anglers in February and March and English anglers have caught them there in December. It won't be long before they are caught intentionally every month of the year as the venue becomes more popular in the future. The other factor controlling growth is availability of food. At present, in the areas where siluro congregate, there are masses of food-fish. The river is rich and is further fertilised by the many sewer outlets that run into it, some of which are untreated, and the carp thrive on this. In fact, in most areas the carp have over-bred and their growth is restricted to three or four pounds which suits the siluro. For years, the Spanish have complained about the over-run of carp spoiling the Ebro and now the siluro is doing them a favour. But even in these highly suitable conditions it is doubtful that the catfish will alter the balance substantially. Other common species in the areas of the siluro are roach and rudd, followed by bass and barbel. It seems to me that there is only one natural thing that can slow down this unprecedented growth rate and that is if the food runs out. At the moment there is no signs of this—you see hundreds of carp everywhere and can catch them all sizes in any spot you chose to try. If siluro does deplete the food fish in its favourite areas it has plenty of river, more than 300 miles, to find pastures new. With all this in mind I have no doubt that *Silurus glanis* has found the best venue it has ever sampled since its existence and in a few years time, barring pollution, I think Spain will hold the world's largest catfish. Whether or not you agree with the fact that one man has a right to do what he did, you must admit it makes a change for man to do a persecuted animal a favour and that is what's happened here.

As far as English anglers are concerned, we have Alastair Nicholson to thank for discovering the venue. Alastair, like myself and some of my friends, is a pioneer—he will respond to snippets of information, learn another language, make the right phone calls and send letters to far away places and then go to a place to try it. He will not only try it, he will find the best spots and then work out the best methods. Most anglers are the opposite. I have 'discovered' several top fisheries on the Continent for English anglers and therefore don't mind admitting that it was Alastair's success that made my friends and I go in search of the Spanish catfish. It took us a year to find the right area and then two holidays to find exactly the right spots and that represents a lot of work. Even though I have done a lot of work in this case, I refuse to name the best areas until Alastair publicly does. I hope Alastair does not do this, because as with Lake Cassien in France, rule-breaking English anglers will probably spoil it. For instance, fishing between mid-night and six in the morning is against the law, yet most English anglers would not hesitate to put permanent bivvies up along the waterside, breaking the rules and drawing attention to themselves. The litter would also be a problem; whilst the Spanish are a dirty lot and they do leave litter, when the banks become strewn with English litter (like Cassien has become) it will stand out and soon the English would not be welcome. The situation is best left as it is—any determined anglers could easily find the place on their own and those that do will deserve what they get.

It was in 1988 that I first fished the Ebro, when Robert Coote, Paul Nash, Stef Zdenek and I spent 10 days fishing different areas and working hard in the extreme heat trying to locate siluro. Although we caught one small one each we returned home with only a little knowledge that was useful. That little piece of information helped us enormously on the next trip and from then onwards we were doing the right things. In fact, we have now got it so sussed out that I would be shocked if we ever returned home without catching some big specimens. We have got to know miles of river and have fished in all sorts of conditions such as severe flood, continuous extreme heat of 40°C every day, and incredible storms that drop several inches of rain and easily blow away a boat out of sight in less than a minute with anchors down. We have caught in all of these conditions.

Although the River Ebro was subjected to much change around 1970 when the series of large dams were completed for generating electricity I always view it as a perfectly natural river. It fluctuates considerably in height, as a normal river would, and varies greatly in depth, which again is quite normal for a river than runs close to, and through, mountainous regions. Depths of up to 100 feet can be found in some places whilst elsewhere there are extensive areas of shallow water. It is these shallow areas that the siluro makes its home with depths between 2 and 20 feet being the best.

Once we had located the siluro we soon discovered that livebaiting was THE method. We continually tried freshly killed dead fish and other baits such as mussels and worms but livebaits easily out-fished all other baits. The silure's main diet appears to be rudd and carp and this source of food is so plentiful that they have become pre-occupied by it. This presents no problem to the catfish angler for as already mentioned carp can easily be caught just about everywhere. Rudd are harder to come by and when available seem to out-fish carp. Some cats are caught by spinning especially at certain times of the year, although legered or paternostered livebaits are generally best. Suitable tackle is as described in the *Tackle & Tactics* section of this book; main line at least 26 pounds, hook links at least 31 pounds, leads between three and six ounces, bank rods of about three pounds test cure with stronger, nine foot rods needed

Paul Nash with a 'tiddler' from the Ebro weighing exactly 20 pounds.

for boat work. A large landing net, gaff, stringers, big weigh sling and suitable scales are the obvious accessories to carry.

Bank and boat fishing is very productive. Sometimes we only fish from the bank but we use a rubber dinghy to row out some of the baits. This doesn't always pay though as there are occasions when the biggest fish of the trip is caught from the margins. What I prefer to do is spread out the rods; one in the margins, one case out a 'comfortable' distance of say 25 yards, and the other taken out by boat. The one furthest out is likely to swing round in the current so I always make this the most downriver rod out of the three (the R/H rod if current is flowing left to right). To combat the effects of flow and debris I put a heavier lead on this rod in combination with the smallest bait I am going to use.

As far as rigs are concerned I now always link leger—I have tried paternoster in Spain and France and I don't find it works as well. I always use a long hook link of about three feet and invariably fit a polyball to keep the bait working. I now prefer to make a hole through the centre of the polyball and actually put it on the hooklink, rather than tie it to the hook as we used to do. It cannot tangle when on the hooklink, and when located by a sliding stop knot (see drawings in Part One) can easily be pushed away when the catfish strikes thereby not possibly inter-fering with the hooking of the catfish. When the siluro are feeding well a polyball makes no difference but when the fishing is hard I have found it definitely helps. But the polyball must be large, big enough to pull the fish upwards as soon as it rests; most anglers do not use one large enough and so its effectiveness is lost. Other methods that most certainly work are, free-roving float fishing just below the surface or in mid-water, and freelining a livebait. Unfortunately both of these methods are difficult to use when other rods are cast into the same vicinity.

As with English catfishing, when a run occurs I strike immediately and as hard as I can. One problem that is often encountered is 'false' runs when a strike results in the loss of what might be a very valuable bait. A lively bait, or a branch drifting down in the current, can give you a run—if in doubt, pick up the rod, open the bail arm and squeeze hard the line between your thumb and forefinger. If the line continues to pay out the chances are it's a cat. In England this would of course result in a dropped run but on the Continent I have done it dozens of times and it doesn't seem to affect these previously un-caught fish. Even at Schnackensee, where the big cats are returned, it doesn't put off a taking fish.

Once a big fish is hooked from the bank it should be played quite hard, remembering always that when a cat swims down with the current, every yard of line will be hard work to recover against the flow. Apart from the odd occasions when you hook a cat in the teeth where it cannot penetrate, these big fish are always well and truly hooked so you can play the fish hard with no fear of it coming off.

At some stage I have to mention two of the main disadvantages in fishing for siluro in Spain. The first is the temperature. The area concerned is said to be the second hottest place in Europe and I believe it. God, I hate heat, but my friend the siluro loves it! In mid-summer, daytime temperatures often reach 40°C and the area becomes a ghost town—even the Spanish can't stand it. It is impossible on some days to be comfortable after 9 am and at mid-day your brolly can melt. Along with the heat comes two other things; millions (and I mean millions) of flies which walk all over every inch of your body for every minute of the day and dust—the terrain is so dry that dust gets everywhere, inside your car, your cooking gear, tackle boxes, clothing etc. making everything filthy. The second disadvantage is thieves. On every occasion except one I have had my car door locks forced open and three times I have caught them inside my car. The police are not in the slightest bit interested and they tell you to give them a good thumping if you catch them again. One most trips we have also had gear stolen from our swims—just turn your back and it's gone. Your gear is being 'eyed up' all the time by visitors (not fisherman) who come back from time to time hoping for an opportunity.

To complete this section on Spain I should like to give an account of a trip we had to the Ebro in October 1989. This will cover any points not fully explained and it was a particularly interesting trip in that we learnt a lot from our mistakes and still managed to catch a fish or two . . .

It was a very late October that Robert Coote, Bob Baldock and myself arrived on the banks of the Ebro with a whole week's fishing in front of us. We'd arranged to meet Peter Ploetz from Germany at the riverside as he was going to join us for a few days. Peter was there but only to tell us that he couldn't fish because his wife was unwell and sadly we waved him goodbye, within a couple of hours of getting there.

The river had been in flood for two weeks previously and was still heavily coloured with quite a flow. The area we chose to fish was about a quarter of a mile wide with the far margins unfishable due to masses of sunken trees. The plan now was for one of us to stay on the bank with the car whilst the other two fished from our boat out in front where we could see each other. This was in case the angler on his own needed a hand with a big fish, or a big Spaniard!

The first afternoon and evening was spent with Bob on the bank and Robert and I on the boat and we didn't have long to wait for the first bite. I had often described to Robert how hard these big Spaniard siluro fight and now it was his turn to find out first hand. The cat had taken a link-legered carp a little before dark and I safely retrieved the other three rods and pulled up one anchor. Instead of fighting downstream

Des John looking happy with this 70 pounder caught on his first visit to the Ebro.

as they often do, this feller insisted on swimming directly towards Bob on the bank. It was all Robert could do to hang on to the 3lb test curve rod bent double with the fish very much in command. When it neared the bank it picked up one of Bob's lines and we then realised that the anchor had moved a little. Originally, we had dropped the anchors on the top edge of a slope so that we were fishing two rods into the main channel and two onto the shallow. This siluro had pulled the boat and anchor over a little towards the channel and the anchor was no longer on the bottom. We were being pulled towards Bob and we had no option but to lift the remaining anchor. Fortunately, the line we'd picked up became free and the cat started to make its way up river. Robert was by now giving line steadily under the tremendous pressure of what was obviously a good fish.

With no anchors down we waved goodbye to Bob as the cat slowly towed us away and upstream. Ten, twenty and thirty minutes passed and by now Robert's arm was really aching and I kept laughing at his moans and groans. Words cannot describe the power of these fish; you have to sample one to believe it and I knew this would happen to Robert sooner or later. His aching arm became an aching shoulder and an hour later an aching back. I don't know why, but the more someone shows amazement at the fighting qualities of these fish the more I laugh and every time Robert groaned I laughed. It was now very dark and we could just about see from the bank that we had been towed upstream at least 200 yards against the strong current. After 1½ hours Robert decided he would have to play it harder and it was shortly after this that we realised just how far we'd been towed. We were now somewhere in the vicinity of a mass of sunken trees some quarter of a mile upstream! There was no point in dropping the anchor at this stage as we didn't know how close to the snags we were. We had no choice but to really pile on the pressure to keep the fish near the surface and at last control of the fight had now changed hands.

Almost two hours after hooking the fish we managed to net it. Robert wasn't in a fit state to row back so I offered, while Robert looked after the huge fish which was now in the bottom of the boat. I had only rowed a few yards when all of a sudden one of the rowlock brackets tore free of the boat and promptly fell overboard. We had no choice but to make for the nearest bank using one oar. Little did we know than that losing that rowlock was soon to cost us one of the biggest catfish of our lives.

We eventually got to the bank and decided to put the fish on a stringer until morning. We tied the boat to a tree, walked up to Bob to explain what had happened and decided that it wasn't worth going out again for the short time that was left so we crashed out on our bed-chairs. A lesson had been learnt—we should have dropped the anchor again as soon as we were clear of Bob's swim.

The next morning, we weighed the beauty of a beast and it went exactly 65 pounds; Robert's first biggy and boy did he know about it. We took lots of stills and a short piece of video before safely returning it to its murky home. We then measured the distance it had towed us— nearly half a mile!

We paid for our first night's quick success by blanking the next day and night. This time it was my turn on the bank with Robert and Bob out in front of me on the boat. No sooner had we all got our baits out when Bob connected with a siluro, but alas it was a small one of about 15 pounds, which had taken a rudd. This was shortly before dark and two hours later I had my first run of the trip. This was on the rod I'd cast close, in the deeper channel, even though I'd expected any action to come on the rod in the shallows that they had taken out for me by boat.

Bob and Robert had heard the run and asked if I'd hooked one. There was no need for me to reply as they could then hear the clutch going steadily. This fish just went and went and went, directly across the river. There was nothing I could do but just hang on as the fish continued to take line slowly but surely. After what seemed an eternity I realised that the fish had run more than 100 yards and my thoughts concentrated on some snags that were about 200 yards out. The fish just kept going while the rod was bent to its full test curve and my heart sank to my boots when I put my fingers around the spool to feel how low the line was. It was nearly empty and this 'thing' must have taken nearly 200 yards! I piled on the pressure by lowering the rod and transferring more strain onto the 26lbs line. This made no difference and for the first time in my life I wondered if I was going to get 'spooled off'. It was too late to call for the boat but I decided to anyway as I wanted the other rods reeled in.

The catfish must have wanted its picture taken because with only about 20 yards of line left on the spool it decided to stop and come back towards me. It took a good 15 minutes to get the fish within about 30 yards when it had the cheek to turn round and do the same thing again. This time it took another 100 yards off the spool and I knew a complete tackle revision was in order for our next trip. This fish was playing me, there was no doubt about it.

Bob and Robert had kindly stopped fishing and come ashore to assist. My other rods were reeled in and Robert handed me a cup of tea—how time flies when you're having fun. By the time an hour had passed Bob started handing out his usual comments, 'Come on Maddocks stop mucking around with this thing and start giving it some welly'! Perhaps he's right I thought and I increased the pressure but after another 15 minutes every muscle in my body hurt so I handed the rod to Bob to keep him quiet. I enjoyed the ten minutes rest and another cup of

Pedro Alamansa lives on the banks of the Ebro and returns all his siluro, like the 70 pounder pictured here. Pedro has formed a local club and has managed to get some laws passed to help protect the catfish.

tea after which Bob handed the rod back with the cat still the same distance out. 'Feels a good one' was all he said.

On paper all fights seem the same so I'll end by saying that we eventually landed the siluro after nearly two hours—it weighed 74 pounds and beat my personal best by five pounds. In the torchlights we all thought the fish was a lot bigger and to this day Bob reckons that this cat is still the most impressive fish he's ever seen. As soon as the fish was safely retained Bob and Robert went back out again and it wasn't long before Bob connected with a big cat which had taken a small carp. I was well pleased when I'd heard that Bob had played the fish for 1½ hours. This was his first really big catfish and I knew he 'blamed' us for the excessive playing time, but now he'd had a long struggle too.

Bob's fish weighed 60 pounds and we tried to photograph the 74 and 60 together but it didn't work out. Besides there being too many cameras for Robert to handle we also had several pairs of shifty Spanish eyes looking at the cats and our gear!

Only three days had gone and already we'd all beaten our personal bests. We continued to catch and the next three days produced cats of 14lbs for Robert, 39, 32, and 26 for Bob and I managed siluro of 44, 34 and two doubles.

We were really enjoying ourselves even though it was very hard work; it was a struggle to catch enough livebaits of the right size and every day we were going two miles away to catch them. This sometimes meant completely packing all our gear into the car only to re-tackle again later in the same spot. With only one day left we made the usual phone calls and arranged to stay another two days.

The main reason for wanting to stay extra time was that I'd hoped to show Robert and Bob an area a few miles away that I'd discovered on my last trip which I'd nicknamed 'The Orchard'. Ever since I first saw this area I really fancied it but Pedro, the local expert that we'd got to know well, said there was no big ones in that area. I told the lads that Pedro might be right because when I tried it just before leaving on the last trip I had non-stop action with 12 cats, including three 30's, but no big ones. I shall never forget those few hours the cats went mad; everytime I got a bait in the water I had a run until eventually I ran out of bait. And the noise—there were literally hundreds of siluro on the feed in the shallows in front of Paul Nash and myself and we couldn't hear each other speak for the incredible splashing and clooping noises as they were chasing around. Catfishing is so different abroad from the U.K.—you see the fish, you hear them, *and you catch them!*

And so we moved to spent the last two or three days on a completely different area of the river.

After replenishing the keepnets and ourselves the first 24 hours or so was spent with Bob set-up on the bank and Robert and I out on

This 30 and 20 pounder were part of a twelve fish catch when the siluro went on a feeding spree.

the boat. No sooner had we cast out and sat back in the boat to enjoy a cup of tea when Robert had an absolute cracker of a run. The cups of tea went flying as all hell let loose on the boat. Immediately upon hooking the cat it decided to swim straight at the boat, and that it did, passing underneath just as I had one of the anchors half way up. We were now fishing a much shallower, faster flowing area of the river, an average of less than 6 feet, so the fights were going to be much more spectacular. It picked up one of the other lines too but I managed to sort it out while Robert played the fish. I can't remember how long the battle lasted but I think it must have been about 1½ hours before we eventually netted what turned out to be another very big fish.

With the siluro on board we paddled over to where Bob was fishing and weighed the fish in at a colossal 69 pounds. Robert had beat his personal best again—what a trip this was turning out to be.

I was keen to get back out again so the fish was put on a stringer and at first light back we went. As soon as we'd got our baits out it happened again—an immediate run, but this time to one of my rods. The first run took 50 yards and this was repeated several times indicating another biggie. The fight went on and on, one hour, two hours, three hours. This was certainly the biggest catfish I'd ever hooked in my life and my tackle was completely inadequate. The current of the river was the deciding factor, using my tackle to its limit resulted in a stalemate; I could hold the fish but not bring it near enough for netting. For a long time I had the leviathan about 10 feet from the boat and on the surface, but all it had to do was wave its tail in the current to hold its own without getting any more tired.

I was very concerned that it would wear through the hooklink for it was often twisting completely around when I got it on the surface. It was a huge fish, well over 100 pounds and I asked Robert if he thought he could row us to shore by paddling one oar. If I could play it from the bank I could have easily landed it. With one rowlock missing from earlier in the week Robert said that he didn't think he could get us to the bank on his own against the current especially with this thing on the other end of the line. I agreed with him. The only option was to try to increase the pressure on the fish and for the next 30 minutes we tried so hard to get it in the net. Three times we had it three quarters in the net but each time we lifted it, it slipped back over the cord. Eventually my fears became reality when the hooklink succumbed to the abrasion of the cat's teeth and all went slack. We had lost the fish of a lifetime. It was almost certainly one of the original 32 stock fish as it was considerably bigger than anything we'd seen or caught. To this day none of the originals have yet been landed.

Bob finished the session by catching a lovely 53 pounder and so we left the river a very thankful team knowing full well that we had just completed what will always remain one of the greatest fishing adventures ever. We had learnt a lot too, about anchors and inadequate tackle and so I advise anyone trying their hand at this game to use the tackle mentioned earlier in this section of the book; we arrived at it the hard way, you need not.

Silurus glanis, I thank you ...

Please remember — litter loses fishing